Someone Died...
Now What?

A Personal and Professional Perspective
on Coping with

Grief and Loss

Corrie Sirota
M.S.W., P.S.W.

To JF + CS,
memories are pictures
we take with
our heart!

keep up the
great work,
fondly,
Corrie

Cover design by Chris Hennessy

Published by Corrie Sirota

ISBN: 150530248X

ISBN-13: 978-1505302486

In loving memory of my brother, Andy Sirota
June 27, 1962 – December 3, 1988

You are the reason I began my work in the field of loss and bereavement.

You serve as my constant reminder that life happens while we are busy making other plans.

TABLE OF CONTENTS

ACKNOWLEDGMENTS

Writing this book has truly been a labour of love. I am blessed with so many special people in my life. The list of those I want to thank for helping, guiding and encouraging me in order to make this project come to fruition is endless.

First and foremost this book is dedicated to my parents, Sonia and Gerry Sirota. How you have managed to find your way through this tragedy serves as a role model of what true heroes are.

To all my clients – you were brave enough to seek support, courageous enough to share your stories and open enough to recognize that you don't have to grieve alone.

To the Paperman family – your professionalism and compassion continue to serve as a model of how to help people in their time of need.

To Stefani Novick, Anna Stein, Marcy Stein – your brilliance is second to none! I could not have done this without you.

To my family and friends – your belief in my ability to do this was unwavering.

And finally, to my husband Andy and my children, Ashley and Justine - you are my inspiration, my everything. Thank you for believing in me even when I didn't believe in myself.

Most sincerely,

Corrie

GONE

The burial in sub-freezing zero
Laid to rest my all time hero.
The burden of sweet memory
And shock of being lonely.

Gone, our pleasure and plans,
Table for two, holding hands.
Gone, the perfectly poached eggs,
Canoe rides at break of day.

The call of his whistle
When I lost my way.
Gone, the endurance of hospital days,
Fighting the fight, trying to stay.

At the altar
Pledging each vow,
Death did us part.
I ask, what now?

You're there, I'm here,
Nothing is clear.
Keep breathing I know
And ask, what now.

Rona Shefler Heft, 2015

INTRODUCTION

How does one find oneself dealing with death and dying every day?

In my case, I didn't find it; it found me.

The Story Behind the Story

It was December 3, 1988, a Saturday morning, like any other. My husband Andy and I had been married for just six months. I had returned home from working out at the gym. The phone rang. Since we didn't have call display back then, I had no idea who was calling. I answered. And I remember hearing my mother's voice; she was screaming and crying at the same time and I could not make out what she was saying. I asked her to say it again and then I heard the words, "Your brother is dead."

I can't really recall what happened next; I think I started to scream and I passed the phone to Andy. It was as if everything seemed to happen in slow motion. My mother then passed the phone to my father who explained that my brother (whose name is also Andy) had been hit and killed by a car that had jumped the sidewalk during a police chase. My brother was killed on impact. He was twenty-six and my only sibling. "WHAT?" I screamed. "Just come here now," my father said and hung up the phone. We got dressed, jumped into our car and drove in silence.

My life, our lives, would never be the same.

At the time of my brother's death, I had already obtained my social work degree and was working in a community setting, focusing primarily on prevention-type programs. This role also included supervising community services – which placed me in direct contact with people who were searching for various support services. One such program – 'Widow to Widow' – was specifically designed for people who had experienced a death in their family. As I continued to work in this area, I became increasingly concerned by the fact that the community did not seem to have adequate support services available for those in need. Upon identifying this gap, I collaborated with Agence Ometz (formerly known as Jewish Family Services, Montreal, Canada) and together we approached Paperman & Sons Funeral Home (Montreal, Canada) in an effort to obtain some funding to create support groups for individuals dealing with loss and bereavement.

As I embarked on this new initiative, I developed a connection with Paperman and Sons that led to my being offered a position managing their After Care Department. My role was to help families at the very vulnerable time immediately after they had experienced a death. This included assistance with basic tasks, which can be overwhelming to those in mourning, such as completing government forms, connecting families with community resources and filing applications for death certificates. I also offered essential psychosocial support for grief and mourning. This is where my passion for the field of loss and bereavement really began to develop.

I suppose there is something to be said about having experienced a traumatic loss in your own life. It helps ground you and makes you realize what is important and what is not. I LOVE making a difference. I cannot imagine doing any other work. When I learned about a graduate certificate program in Loss and Bereavement being offered at McGill University (Montreal, Canada), I knew this would be the perfect complement to the work in which I was already so invested. The specific theoretical training I received in the program, coupled with my personal and professional experience, was the perfect recipe to secure my place as an expert in the field.

For the past twenty years I have listened to and accompanied thousands of people through their grief journeys. I truly believe in the counselling process and in the individual's own capacity to overcome adversity.

Grief is a *process*, not an event; you will hear me remind you of this throughout the book. It is not a race and it does not keep a schedule. It is this **process** I want to share with you. While I recognize that MY journey is not YOUR journey, each journey shares similar experiences and feelings. To this end, if something I suggest, or any of the tips and hints are helpful, or if even one of the anecdotes resonates with you and gives you some insight into your own situation, then you will be on the road to working through your grief.

My hope is that by the end of this book you will understand how to navigate the grief process, learn how to move forward by giving yourself permission to laugh without guilt and learn how to live after loss. To this end, I offer very concrete tips and guidelines for the practical aspects of dealing with death and mourning.

My role is simply to accompany you through your journey, to help guide, support and provide perspective on a situation that can turn your life inside out and upside down, while at the same time demonstrating how you can go from hopeless to hopeful and believe it's possible.

We can endure much more than we think we can;
all human experience testifies to that. All we need to
do is learn not to be afraid of pain. Grit your teeth

and let it hurt. Don't deny it, don't be overwhelmed by it.
It will not last forever. One day, the pain will be gone
and you will still be there.

Harold Kushner, 2002

A Bit About This Book

By nature I am a very proactive individual, so whenever I hear someone say, "What choice do I have?" I cringe. It actually hurts me to hear this phrase; even though it's posed as a question, it's really a very nihilistic statement. I believe we *always* have choices. Granted, we may have limited choices and we may not like the choices we have, but rest assured they do exist. The minute you say, "What choice do I have?" you give up two essential elements: your power and your control. The experience of loss, which turns your world upside down, is entirely out of your control and that is truly scary. Much of what we think we know and believe to be true may change with the death of a loved one. Whether you have experienced a loss for the very first time or whether you have experienced one before, each loss is unique and the experience brings with it new challenges.

As much as we would desperately like to do so, there is no going back. We need to find our way forward. Sometimes we accomplish this one day at a time and sometimes one hour at a time. How we manage that is a choice. Nowhere in this book will you find me telling you that this process will be easy, but I will tell you unequivocally that it will be worth it.

Life has so much to offer; there is still much more that you can and need to do. It's not about forgetting your loved one and moving on; it's about taking the experience of loss, the memory of the loved one and finding a space for that grief while creating **new normals.** The biggest challenge you face when a loved one dies is to create a future without that person.

Challenges are what make life interesting –
overcoming them is what makes life meaningful.

Joshua Marine

CHAPTER ONE

"GET OVER IT" AND
OTHER STUPID THINGS PEOPLE SAY

We live in an age of disposable public grief, orchestrated on television in living color, with talking heads telling us what we're supposed to think and feel. Shock and horror Tuesday, mourning Wednesday and we're supposed to be over it by Thursday. The sheer repetition of the images of tragedy – falling towers, school shootings, natural disasters – numbs the senses and robs us of genuine grief.

Jack Todd, 2014

Here in the West, we live in a death denying society. That's right, not death-*defying*, but death *denying*. Many of us cannot even use the words death or dead. Instead, we use euphemisms that soften the finality of the term.

Some terms are gentler and help us imagine a passing over to another reality or sphere, such as: 'left us', 'laid to rest', 'eternal rest', 'went to a new life' and 'the great beyond'. By far the most common phrase, 'passed away', is probably wishful thinking; don't we all wish that our loved ones and those close to us will simply *pass on* with a gentle and painless departing? Some euphemisms have a religious connotation: 'gone to heaven', 'gone home', 'went to his eternal reward', 'G-d took him', 'he met his maker', 'was translated into glory' or 'is on the heavenly shores'. Others are meant to be funny, perhaps to break the tension or the gravity of the loss, or, when one is more further removed from the situation: 'croaked', 'kicked the bucket', 'pushing up the daisies', 'cashed in', 'that's all she wrote'. And still others are irreverent, verging on the morbid, perhaps aimed at thumbing one's nose at death: 'bit the dust', 'annihilated', 'rubbed out', 'snuffed' and, one that's not only descriptive, but accurate, 'six feet under'. My personal favourite, 'expired' sounds as if the person were a type of yogurt!

Why do we do this? Why is there a need for such indirect language? Usually out of fear, discomfort or denial in order to avoid facing what has actually occurred. In my experience, no one sets out to dismiss your loss or add to your pain during this difficult time. In fact, they are likely trying to be supportive, but are often relying on their own limited background related to loss and lack the necessary skills and understanding to know just what to say. Instead, they bombard you with platitudes. Widows, widowers, couples who have been together for many years or even just a short time, parents who have miscarried, children who lose parents at a young age and children who lose parents to illness, parents who lose children, friends who lose friends – all experience loss and bereavement and all go through the mourning process. Below are some of the platitudes I have heard shared with the bereaved I have counselled. All these sentiments are well intentioned, but actually exacerbated the pain and grief of the loss.

- "In time you will feel better."

- "At least he/she didn't suffer."

- "I know just how you feel."

- "When one door closes another door opens."

- "There is something better."

- To the widow: "What are you going to do with all your free time now?" or "Join the club."

- In reference to miscarriage: "You can always have another one," or "At least you know you can get pregnant."

- In reference to a young man who was killed on a street corner at 2:00 AM: "What was he doing out at that hour anyway?"

- "What are you so sad about? He was 91. He lived a long life."

- "Well you know it's normal for your grandmother to be upset. She buried a child. That's not normal."

- "You buried your mother. That's the natural order of things, so what are you so upset about?"

- On the 7th month anniversary of Joan's father's death, a friend said, "It's been 7 months; I don't understand why you're still so upset."

- Bob, upon hearing someone rationalize his 94-year-old father's death, responded, "But he was my father, my best friend."

The classic line that is often used when something sad, bad, difficult or painful has happened is ***"It was meant to be"***, as if such a platitude will magically make it all better.

Some people will say many things; some people will say nothing at all. People tend to forget that the deceased is someone's husband, someone's sister, someone's child, regardless of age, regardless of the circumstance of their death. The time you had with your loved one on Earth – a few months or ninety-four years

– is irrelevant to the indelible mark he or she leaves on your heart. I learned a long time ago that only if I was capable of waving a magic wand that would bring back the loved one would I be truly "making it better." Unfortunately, I have not yet learned to do this.

> *Everyone experiences loss differently; remembering that sometimes 'nothing helps' can stop you from blaming yourself in the midst of your grief.*

> Will Schwalbe, 2013

Even the greeting card industry puts out condolence cards that seem to have nothing to do with death; a frustrated colleague pointed out that she wished she could find just one card that did not depict palm trees, sand and sunny skies, as if to say, *"Our deepest condolences on the death of your loved one and have a good time in Maui."*

> *The reality is that you will grieve forever. You will not 'get over' the loss of a loved one; you will learn to live with it. You will heal and you will rebuild yourself around the loss you have suffered. You will be whole again but you will never be the same. Nor should you be the same, nor would you want to.*

> Elisabeth Kübler-Ross & David Kessler, 2005

CHAPTER TWO

GRIEF IS A PROCESS, NOT AN EVENT

Grief is a tidal wave that overtakes you, smashes down upon you with unimaginable force, sweeps you up into its darkness, where you tumble and crash against unidentifiable surfaces, only to be thrown out on an unknown beach.

Stephanie Ericson, 1993

The Difference Between Grief and Mourning

Grief is really the internal process – the thoughts and feelings you have when someone you love dies. Mourning is the act of taking the internal feelings of grief and expressing them externally through rite and ritual.

In the West, we are not encouraged to openly express our feelings of grief. Because Western culture and religions regard death as final we are faced with a "get over it" attitude. It is precisely this attitude that makes the grief process so personal and challenging.

By contrast, Eastern faiths such as Buddhism and Hinduism incorporate concepts around death and dying into daily life. They are communal and familial, highly ritualized and deeply personal.

5

Although there are a myriad of traditions and rich symbolism rooted in each culture, there is no ordained way to grieve.

> *Grief is not a disorder, a disease or a sign of weakness. It is an emotional, physical, and spiritual necessity, the price you pay for love. The only cure for grief is to grieve.*

Rabbi Earl Grollman, 1993

Myths Surrounding the Grieving Process

While the grief experience is unique to each person, there are a number of common questions that I am frequently asked. How long should it take to get over a death? Will I have to live with this pain for the rest of my life? When will the hurt go away? How am I going to live without him/her the rest of my life?

In an effort to answer these questions, I will explore a number of common myths surrounding grief and loss.

Myth #1: Everybody grieves in the same way.

No two people grieve in the same way; it is an entirely individual process. I have, many times, used the analogy that grief is like a fingerprint or a snowflake. I have long since removed the sentence, "I know how you feel" from my lexicon – because I don't. No one does. Having lost a brother, I can understand some of the challenges one experiences but I don't know how anyone else feels nor does anyone know how I feel.

Myth #2: Grief will go away if you ignore it.

No, plain and simple. If you ignore it, it will always be under the surface and will manifest itself in other ways. Grief is like a pressure cooker; it can boil up inside you and explode. It will be reflected in your actions, your behaviour and your health. Try to find an appropriate place and space in which to share it. Support in the form of group or individual counselling can serve as an important step in working through the process of grief.

Myth #3: If you don't cry it means you didn't care about your loved one.

If you're not a crier you will not naturally become one. I recall meeting with Paul, an eight year-old boy whose mother had died suddenly. Everyone around him kept encouraging him to cry. When I asked about what type of child Paul was and if he tended to cry over things, I was told no, not really. So I then asked if anyone had told him it was okay *not* to cry. It seemed to me he may have been receiving a very strong message that the way in which he was grieving was wrong. There is no right or wrong way to grieve.

Myth #4: Children don't grieve.

If you are able to feel, you are able to grieve. Children often become the forgotten grievers. I have experienced this in my practice as well as in my personal life. Friends of mine were dealing with the sudden death of their friends' son, a beautiful six-year-old boy who had been tragically killed in an accident. The child was the best friend of their own six-year-old daughter. The death was a shock to all. I have heard my friend tell this story several times in great detail as part of her own grieving process. Many, many times she has repeated how this has affected her. This was done in front of her six year old whom I have observed just sitting quietly; the child has never been asked how she feels. Usually, when her mother gets to a certain point in the story, Jessica will get up and quietly leave the room. What must it feel like for her to hear that her friend loved her so much and now he's gone? Or that they were supposed to have been playing together when the accident happened? I finally spoke to my friend and offered some gentle suggestions about how she might approach the situation, highlighting how their daughter was truly a forgotten griever. Chapter Eleven will offer greater insight into this concept.

Myth #5: A sudden death is worse than a death resulting from a long-term illness.

I am often asked, "What's worse – a sudden death or one after a long term illness?" My response is *neither*. It's not a contest! Both are difficult and have their unique challenges.

Myth #6: Time heals all wounds.

While many people may agree with this statement, it is very difficult to tell you as you are going through the grieving process that you will feel better in time. Perhaps a more honest and realistic approach is to say, *It's not a matter of how much time it will take, but what you do with the time that matters.* By this I mean that even though grief can be compared to an open wound that eventually heals, the scar will still remain. The healing process is a natural part of life, but it is your choice whether you want to take an active part in this process or simply watch from the sidelines.

Myth #7: It's a good idea to dispose of the deceased's belongings as soon as possible.

There is no magic formula as to when the best time to do this would be. You are more likely to feel overwhelmed just after the death and there will most likely be a strong sense of attachment to belongings at that time. Donating your loved one's belongings is an important part of the healing process and can only be done when the surviving family members have found a way to make a distinction between the deceased and his or her material items.

Myth #8: It's harder to cope with the death of a relative than the death of a friend.

A loss is a loss. You cannot and should not compare

situations; no one mourner has it better or worse, easier or harder. It is the meaningfulness of the relationship one attaches to the loss that contributes to how one feels about it.

Myth #9: After a year you should be over with your mourning.

Again, grief is not a race; there is no finish line. You don't get over it; you learn to live with it. Be open-minded. You need to give yourself time to recover.

Myth #10: If you have to seek counselling it means there is something wrong with you.

I often hear clients say, "I think I'm going crazy." You're not going crazy; you're grieving. The roller coaster of emotions really wreaks havoc on your thought processes, which causes you to question your ability to make decisions. I often receive calls from family members expressing great concern about their surviving parent who is grieving the death of his or her spouse. When I ask them to describe the behaviour, they will invariably say that the surviving parent has been crying a lot. My next question is, "How long has it been since your mother died?" They answer, "Two weeks," and then I follow up with the question, "How long had your parents been married?" They reply, "40, 50 + years," so I say, "What *should* they be doing?" Everybody can use a little help from time to time. Dealing with death is no exception. Check your local hospital, community or social services centre in your area for support.

The Reality of Grief

> It has been said, 'time heals all wounds.' I do not agree. The wounds remain. In time, the mind, protecting its sanity, covers them with scar tissue and the pain lessens. But it is never gone.
>
> Rose Kennedy

The thing about grief is that it's always there; sometimes it's more pronounced and at the forefront of your thoughts, and at other times it lies just low enough beneath the surface that you are able to function without it interfering in your daily life. The thing that many people don't understand is that even though many of us are able to put on the facade of normalcy, GRIEF IS EVER PRESENT; some of us just know how to hide it better than others. Then, all of a sudden, something will happen to "trigger" strong feelings to emerge (please see Chapter Eight, *Triggers,* for a full explanation and coping strategies). Whether it is a song, a smell, a food, a television show or a date that looms large on the calendar and stirs thoughts and emotions back up to the surface, a trigger can be powerful and even overwhelming. It can bring you face to face with your grief and pain, and the only way to deal with grief is to grieve. Don't fight it; embrace it. We feel pain, sadness, anger and loneliness because we had someone in our lives who was worthy of evoking all these emotions in us. Consider that relationship a gift!

Pearl's husband died at the age of 97. Pearl was 86. She knew that when people heard her story they would immediately think that she could not have much to be sad about. After all, he had lived for 97 years! She knew she was fortunate to have had him for so long, but from her perspective, they had been married for 68 years and she didn't remember ever being without him! It didn't matter how old he was. She missed him!

In order to work through a loss you must understand the journey faced by a mourner. Personally I don't want to get hung up on the semantics. Whether it's a stage, a task or a phase, it's a process that you do not "get over"; rather, you need to pass through it, in your own time, in your own way. The mourning process is like a roller coaster – it has high and low periods, peaks and valleys. It is not linear; it does not get better or worse with time (although it does get easier for some). It changes constantly and, as such, many grievers may find themselves consistently experiencing a variety of emotions. There are numerous theories about grieving, many of which describe the process beginning with shock and denial and running through several stages, ending with some form of acceptance. Acceptance is probably the trickiest stage of all, primarily because it looks very different for everyone. I would contend that even though you might find yourself experiencing a certain degree of acceptance, this may be on a strictly intellectual level, and therefore, you can find yourself back in disbelief that a particular event, loss or ending has actually occurred.

Understanding the Phases, Stages and Tasks of Grieving

A number of theories have been developed to demonstrate the process of grieving, as illustrated in the following table:

Stages: Kübler-Ross (1969)	Phases: Parkes (1972)	Tasks: Worden (1981)	Processes of Mourning: Rando (1991)	Duel Processes: Stroebe & Schut (1995)
Denial	Shock vs. Reality	Accept reality of loss	Reorganize the loss	
Anger	Protest vs. Experience	Work through the pain of grief	React to the separation	Loss orientation
Bargaining	Disorganization vs. Adjustment	Adjust to an environment in which the deceased is missing.	Recollect and re-experience the deceased	&
Grief		Emotionally relocate the deceased & move on with life	Relinquish old attachments	Restoration orientation
Acceptance				

While each theory has its own unique language to describe the stages of grieving, they share similar traits. There are three responses that present most frequently in my clients.

Denial / Shock

As Elizabeth Kübler-Ross and a number of other grief theorists have cited, some sense of denial is the first stage of the grief process. However you might find yourself stuck in this place without even knowing it - a denial that you are in denial of sorts. This type of denial can be summarized as:

Didn't

Even

KNow

I

Am

Lying

This speaks volumes about how people perceive and live through their challenges. If they don't really acknowledge them, then perhaps they don't exist. So, my question is, "Is that working for you?" It's true that if you face your sadness, the loss, and the truth about how you feel, it may be too painful, too hurtful, and too overwhelming to bear. But denial only works for so long and then sometime, somewhere, somehow, it has a funny, but, not-so-funny way of creeping up on you (usually when you least expect it) and, BOOM, you find yourself in crisis and you have no idea why.

Throughout my time as the After Care Professional at the funeral home, I met with thousands of families who had experienced the death of a loved one. More often than not, when we sat down to discuss the deceased, I heard instead about long unresolved issues of sibling rivalries, miscarriages, deaths that had occurred twenty, thirty, forty years prior and other stories of loss. It doesn't go away; nobody escapes grief. People tend to do a great job of hiding it, sweeping it under the rug, so to speak. With every loss, however, there are both positive and negative feelings and when we deny those feelings they have to go somewhere. They are sublimated and end up expressing themselves in risk-taking behaviours, physical ailments, eating disorders, self-medication and a range of other means that help numb the pain.

When you experience an ending – loss of a job, break up, divorce, or a death – your default reaction commonly tends to be that of shock/denial or disbelief. It's your emotional and physical strategy for holding it together so that you can otherwise function. I have met numerous people who recounted, when asked, "How did you manage to make it through the funeral?" that it was like an out-of-body experience. While they physically went through the motions, their mind and spirit were not really present. It's an interesting trick that your psyche does for you as a protective mechanism, as a way to ensure that you are able to get through the first stage of grieving without becoming entirely paralyzed or completely unglued. It seems to me that there is always a little part of you that remains in denial; if you really accepted that the unimaginable or unthinkable has actually happened it would be just too painful to absorb. So while a part of you recognizes the loss on an intellectual level there is an emotional distancing that helps you to cope through each day.

Anger

While not always the case, once the numbness of the loss has dissipated (after approximately three months, or, as I like to call it "when the casseroles stop coming"), you might find yourself experiencing a period of anger. One client, Patty, described her anger at her husband for dying as, "I forgive him but I don't." You are angry at everything: the doctors, your spouse, siblings, children, parents, your employer, your friends, anyone and everyone who might be remotely connected to the loss. You might also feel abandoned and alone. Your life has been forced to change drastically, on top of which there might be a number of new and pressing responsibilities that have been thrust upon you. It is not uncommon for some mourners to resent others who haven't experienced a loss. Some mourners ask, "Why me?" Anger can also be seen as a cover for sadness, particularly for men, who have learned that it is far more socially acceptable to display feelings of anger as opposed to sadness. Crisis brings out the best and the worst in families, and often it can be downright brutal!

Sometimes people turn the anger inward for being in this very situation. You might be angry because you somehow should be able to figure this all out on your own, but you can't. For those of you who tend to think this way, keep in mind that there are things that are within your control, but much that is not. For the things over which you have no control, remember that no matter how angry you may become, absolutely no amount of anger will change the situation. For that which is in your control, you've got to change it yourself! Once you recognize that anger is part of the process, you can stop feeling so bad and learn to find a way to manage it.

What can you do with your anger?

- Admit you're angry; don't suppress it. Try not to blame someone else for your anger (even though it might be easier to do so).

- Identify the reasons for your anger.

- Determine what it is you expect to accomplish from being angry.

- Speak out; talk about your anger with someone you trust – a family member, a friend, or a professional.

- Practice relaxation techniques: meditation, breathing techniques or yoga.

- Exercise. Physical activity helps reduce your stress level. A word of caution – if you have not recently done so or do not exercise regularly, make sure to have a physical assessment so that you don't injure yourself.

Consider how much more you often suffer from your anger and grief, than from those very things for which you are angry and grieved.

Marcus Antonius

Grief / Sadness (Also Known as The Mourning Period)

It is very easy to throw yourself a never-ending pity party. Whoever came up with the term "wallowing" certainly knew how comforting it is to simply sit back and feel sorry for yourself; it can feel downright therapeutic. You do need to allow yourself time to grieve, to cry and to feel the pain of the loss. Nevertheless, it is virtually impossible to sustain such an intense level of sadness for an indefinite period of time. Our nervous systems won't physically allow us to do so. Therefore if you find yourself unable to find even brief periods of relief, please contact your doctor or seek supportive counselling. How to deal with your sadness will be addressed in more detail in Chapter Four.

One final note on the grief process; grief can look a lot like depression, however, these are two very distinct concepts. The table on the following page was developed by John M. Schneider (2012) as a guide to help you understand the difference between grief and depression:

Issue	Grief	Depression
Loss	There is a recognized loss.	A specific loss may or may not be identified.
Cognitive Schemas	Focus is on the death. Preoccupation with the deceased, implications of loss, the future.	Focus is on the self. Persistent distorted and negative perception of self.
Dreams, Fantasies or Imagery	Vivid, clear dreams, sometimes of the loss; dreamer feels comforted.	Negative imagery that contributes to negative perception of self.
Physical	Modulated physical response; the body is allowed to collapse and person admits exhaustion.	Un-modulated response: Bodily damage and increased vulnerability to illness - via lack of sleep, anorexia or weight gain, unnecessary physical risks.
Spiritual	A connection felt to something beyond, e.g. G-d; continued dialogue with emotions allows challenges to previously held beliefs.	Especially a year or more past the loss, a persistent failure to find meaning; focus on "why me" and unfairness of loss; no answers to questions.
Emotional Status	Variable shifts in mood from anger to sadness to more normal status in same day.	Fixed: withdrawal, despair, reports feeling immobilized or stuck; difficult to "read" emotions.
Responses	Responds to warmth, touch, reassurance.	Responds to promises and urging or is unresponsive.
Pleasure	Variable restriction of pleasure.	Persistent restriction of pleasure.
Attachment Behaviour	Feels reassured by the presence of close friends or someone who is willing to listen to their story.	Loss of connection with self and/or others.

In his speech, *The Art of Happiness*, The Dalai Lama explains his perspective on the grief process:

> *Initially, of course, feelings of grief and anxiety are a natural human response to a loss. But if you allow these feelings of loss and worry to persist, there's a danger; if these feelings are left unchecked, they can lead to a kind of self-absorption. A situation where the focus becomes your own self. And when that happens you become overwhelmed by the sense of loss, and you get a feeling that it's only you who is going through this. Depression sets in. But in reality, there are others who will be going through the same kind of experience. So, if you find yourself worrying too much, it may help to think of the other people who have similar or even worse tragedies. Once you realize that, then you no longer feel isolated, as if you have been single pointedly picked out. That can offer you some kind of condolence.*

The Dalai Lama, 1988

Regardless of whether grief is described in stages, phases or tasks, one aspect is quite clear; grief is a process, not an event, and as such you will need to find your own way through the experience in your own time.

CHAPTER THREE

FEELINGS AREN'T RIGHT OR WRONG, THEY JUST ARE

Grief is like a snowflake – sometimes it comes one flake at a time, other times it comes like a blizzard. It melts away but it always comes back. Just as each snowflake is unique, each person experiences grief in their own way.

Julia Cook, 2012

What are Normal Reactions to Grief?

Grief affects people holistically – emotionally, physically, cognitively and behaviourally.

Common emotional reactions to grief can include:

- Denial

- Numbing and detachment

- Disorientation and perceptual distortions and, in extreme cases, disassociation and amnesia

- Anger

- Sadness

- Fear and anxiety

- Guilt

So here's where I remind you again that you are not going crazy! It can be very overwhelming and scary when you can't seem to get a handle on your emotions. Nevertheless, as much as the media has portrayed various examples of grieving there is not one definitive way to feel.

Common physical reactions to grief can include:

- Physical shock which can include perspiration, nausea, tremors, uncontrollable crying or laughter

- Exhaustion / Fatigue

- Gastrointestinal problems

- Allergies, skin eruptions

- Vascular, cardiovascular and muscular problems

- Fluctuation in blood pressure. I have had clients who describe feeling as though they were having a heart attack during the early or acute stages of the grief process. This can be an over identification with the deceased related to the manner in which they died. Any pervasive or persistent pains should be checked out by your family physician.

Common cognitive reactions to grief can include:

- Emotional outbursts and mood swings

- Difficulty concentrating

- Confusion

- Impaired judgment

- Memory lapses

Grieving is hard work and can rapidly exhaust you. As you navigate through each day in your new reality, you may find yourself feeling entirely depleted. You may also experience hearing the voice of the deceased and feeling him or her around you. This is not your mind playing tricks on you; this is a legitimate part of the grieving process.

Common behavioural reactions to grief can include:

- Compulsive, repetitive automatic actions

- Aggression

- Irritability

- Situational depression or withdrawal

- Sleeping difficulties or changes in sleep patterns

- Change in libido or other appetites

The bottom line is that you know yourself best. In my practice, I tend to look for significant changes in behaviour according to three major criteria:

1. **Frequency.** How often does the behaviour occur? All day? A few times a day? Let's take crying for example; how often do you cry? Are there periods of time when you don't cry? Is crying a typical reaction and/or a coping mechanism for you?

2. **Intensity.** How extreme is the behaviour or feeling? Do you cry uncontrollably?

3. **Duration.** How long has the behaviour and/or emotion lasted? One day? One week? One month? If a loved one

has died, you may find yourself crying on and off forever and that's perfectly normal. However, if your crying is interfering with functioning on a daily basis this may indicate a more pervasive problem that requires additional support.

Strong Emotions

Of all the emotions that are expressed to me, the one that resonates throughout my practice is the feeling of sadness. A number of clients describe their feelings of sadness as a prevailing feeling of loneliness. There is the transition from being a couple to being single, the transition of losing a close friend, losing a child or losing a sibling. With each loss, you lose a part of yourself. There are the feelings of isolation, the sense of living in a world where no one truly understands your grief. These feelings can best be described by the following sentiments of those whom I have counselled:

- "When I wake up in the morning I feel a pain in my heart."

- "I have everything and I am still alone."

- "When I am with people I'm okay, but when I get home the emptiness is killing me."

- "Who is going to love me like this?"

- "I miss the love."

- "Why does it hurt so much?"

- "It's the **finality** of death that adds to the pain. Sleeping alone, eating alone – we did everything together."

- "I have lots of people to do something with, but *no one* to do nothing with."

At a widow support group I facilitated, Grace shared with the group that she no longer enjoyed getting her hair done. *"Why?"* asked Sheila. *"When I was married, and I came home from having it done,"* Grace explained, *"I always had someone there to tell me I looked nice. And now there's no one there."*

Sometimes you just want to stay in bed, pull the covers over your head and not come out. EVER. I have had this discussion with numerous clients and have told each one that if lying in bed and feeling sad was going to make things better, I would highly recommend doing it for as long as you need to or longer, but it doesn't change a thing. And while it might feel good it really just delays the inevitable – having to go out and face the world. Sitting around feeling sorry for yourself is a complete and utter waste of time – it gives you nothing, nada, zero, zilch! So why do we do it? Because we need to. You need to take some time to wallow, to feel bad for yourself, about your situation, to mourn the loss, to cry, to scream, to yell, to hit (preferably a pillow or a punching bag). Letting it out helps you through the grieving process. Holding on so tightly without ever allowing yourself to feel will only delay it. So feel free to throw a pity party – we all deserve some time to feel sorry for ourselves every now and again, but don't overdo it either because every party (even a bad one) must come to an end.

In her 80's, Betty's eighty-five-year-old husband had died and she said to me, "Everybody keeps telling me I've got to be strong. What do I have to do, lift a refrigerator?"

There seems to be a need for a facade that demonstrates your strength; you must be strong, as if strength alone was going to help you cope. Surviving the loss of a loved one is proof enough of your strength; however, it does not inoculate you against loneliness.

The burial process and visits to the cemetery can, and often do, elicit strong emotions. It seems mourners, friends and family generate tremendous ambivalence, discomfort and confusion about going to the cemetery. The customs around burial and visitation conjure up all sorts of feelings and there is often confusion over whether to visit and when to visit. Below are all statements and stories shared with me about going or not going to the cemetery:

- "I am feeling awkward; what do I say? Who's watching me?"

- "I hate the sound of the earth on the casket."

- "I am at the cemetery so much that I feel like a cemetery connoisseur."

Sara's son died at two months of age. He was buried at a section called Weeping Willow. Sara found herself going to place a blanket on the grave of her son on a cold evening out of fear that he was feeling cold.

Some clients express feeling guilty about not being able to go to the cemetery and others feel compelled to go regularly. There really is no right or wrong – it is a very personal decision that only you can make. Keep in mind that many people were raised to think that a cemetery is no place for children. Hollywood, children's literature, books and Western culture in general all depict cemeteries with such a creepy and foreboding atmosphere that it is no wonder most people fear them.

Yet in the spring and summer, a cemetery can be a beautiful place to reflect upon your experience of loss and to remember your loved one. Do what is right for you. Try not to let others define how often and/or if you need to go to the cemetery. The fact is, no one is obligated to go to the cemetery; it is an entirely personal and voluntary choice that only you can make. Make the experience meaningful to you. Take control of that choice. If you are apprehensive about going, talk to someone about what scares you. Where does that fear stem from? What or whom do you need to support you? Some mourners prefer to go to the cemetery alone, while others prefer to go with another loved one. The decision is entirely up to you.

Susan has actually refused to go 'visit' her grandparents. She refuses not because she didn't love them and doesn't miss them; on the contrary, she adored them and really misses them but can't stand the idea of seeing them as a plot of earth.

I liked my husband Andy's aunt very much; she was a warm lady. I like Andy's cousins; they are good people. When Andy's aunt died, I thought it only proper that, to pay my respects, I assist in the burial. As is our custom, I put some earth on the casket. When the service was over, as is typical of all funerals, we formed a line to allow the mourners to walk past. As I watched the mourners pass, I thought, "How do we place our loved ones in the ground and then turn and walk away?" Then I realized, I was not doing it for myself, I was doing it in honour of my aunt. Assisting in the burial is one of the greatest acts of loving kindness you can do because you are doing something for someone who can never say thank you. Therefore, even though your presence at the cemetery can be emotionally difficult, never underestimate the power of this experience and the impact that your presence has on others.

A Tip for Visiting the Cemetery

Melanie tells me she finds it helpful to check the obituary notices before going to the cemetery for a visit. She prefers to know if there will be a crowd because she does not want to show up and find herself surrounded by a large number of people.

Sometimes you will never know the true value of a moment until it becomes a memory.

Dr. Seuss

CHAPTER FOUR

STOP BEING "SHOULD ON"

Peace is a result of retraining your mind to process life as it is rather than as you think it should be.

Wayne Dyer, 2009

I have been told by a number of clients, *"I don't like going out in public – I feel judged." "Judged by whom?"* I ask. *"Everyone,"* they reply. Know this: you can't win! No matter what you do, according to someone or to everyone, you are doing it wrong. That is to say, a griever fears that if he or she looks too happy people will think that he or she never really cared for the deceased. Conversely, if they look too sad, then people tend to regard them with pity. My suggestion? Go out and do whatever you need to do to cope, to grieve, to mourn – because people will always have an opinion about how you should behave.

When a close family friend died, Sally was upset because the surviving spouse seemed to find another partner just a little too fast. She expressed how inappropriate she felt it was and questioned the surviving spouse's loyalty to his partner. Shortly thereafter, another close family friend died and that surviving spouse was so distraught he could barely find the energy to leave his house. Sally then commented on how terrible it was that the surviving spouse wasn't going out at all.

I immediately pointed out the contradiction in the same basic scenario, questioning Sally about what she thought the 'proper' way to comfort oneself in this situation would be. Should the surviving spouse go out? Not go out? Whose business is this? This underscores my point that there is never really any *one* right way to grieve. The right way is the way that works for you; whatever feels comfortable and right (providing it's not dangerous – as that creates a whole host of other issues).

In my experience, it may seem as though virtually everybody around you is trying to tell you exactly what you *SHOULD* or *SHOULD NOT* do. Whether this is out of concern or any other motivation, whether you do or don't follow these suggestions, you might find yourself feeling a sense of guilt.

Guilt comes in many forms, shapes and sizes. Mourners express their guilt in the following ways:

- "I really should call my mother more."

- "I never got to say good-bye."

- "I never feel I'm doing enough."

- "I don't feel I say what needs to be said."

- "We didn't get a chance to do what we should have done: we were *just gonna*" (e.g. go on vacation, etc...).

What's So Bad About Guilt?

Guilt is all around us. It can consume your daily thoughts and be as hard to part with as your favourite old sweater. For many people, many aspects of life are driven by guilt. It can creep up on you if you're procrastinating about doing an unpleasant task or it can blindside you following the untimely death of a loved one.

Guilt can also be a heavy load to carry; you can find yourself easily manipulated by the pressure of knowing or doing something just because you feel bad. Guilt becomes particularly problematic when you find yourself setting unrealistically high expectations for yourself.

Guilt can also have some positive aspects, such as:

- drawing you closer to others.

- helping you make choices and decisions for the good of others.

- teaching you about yourself.

- helping you identify your moral compass.

  Grief is not as heavy as guilt, but it takes more away from you.

  Veronica Roth, 2012

Where Does Guilt Come From?

Guilt can stem from an over acceptance of the burden of responsibility. While the pang of guilt can be precisely the appropriate response in a situation where you have actually done something hurtful or disrespectful, you may run the risk of using this powerful emotion as an excuse for your behaviour rather than truly owning and accepting your behaviour and being able to move forward. For some, guilt is a safety net which is relied upon to maintain a status quo pattern of actions and behaviours. There are, indeed, many people who *always* feel guilty. From the moment they wake up in the morning they feel guilty and that feeling continues throughout the day and then they go to bed feeling guilty. They remember all the things they did not do that day that they *should have* done. They remember their real or imagined misdeeds toward others in their lives (parents, children or friends) and become so consumed by guilt that they are immobilized. This too can be seen as over-identification. In this case, guilt is not helpful or empowering, but, paralyzing.

When grieving the loss of a loved one, if guilt does become immobilizing, you need to *re-frame the function* that guilt serves in your life. You need to recognize that the purpose of guilt is not, ultimately, to make you feel bad for your wrong doings. Even though it might be the price you pay for caring, you need not be afraid of your feelings. Guilt can lead you to that revolving door of what you "would or should have done", but, properly channeled, it can lead to more productive measures. While that process is one that might take a lifetime to fully master, it is well worth it; it is one that reaps benefits for you and for those around you. Feeling guilty is, therefore the beginning of the process, not the end.

Strategies for Handling Guilt (adapted from Dr. Dorothy J. Marron's report on guilt):

- **Acknowledge the Feelings.** Denying guilt prevents you from getting to the root of the problem.

- **Accept the Feelings.** This may involve unlearning what you were taught as a child. It is okay to feel guilty just as it is okay to feel angry, jealous or scared. These are natural human responses to certain situations. Everyone experiences them at some point in their lifetime. Once you accept these feelings you are then able to choose if you want to do something about them.

- **Forgive Yourself.** Let go of past misdeeds that still cause guilty feelings. If you have hurt someone, apologize and move on. Letting go of your guilt is a gift that you give to yourself and everyone in your life. It will make you a happier and more pleasant person. It is obviously trickier when the person about whom you feel guilty is deceased. In this instance, sharing your feelings (speaking to a loved one at his or her grave, writing a letter, speaking with a trusted friend, family member or counsellor) can be invaluable in making amends.

- **Set Reasonable Expectations.** You might often feel guilty when you fail to live up to your own or someone else's expectations of you. Refuse to accept unreasonable demands made by others. You will reduce feelings of failure and the subsequent guilt that follows.

- **Maintain Perspective.** Often you believe that you are powerful enough to have made something change over which, in reality, you had absolutely no control. So when you are feeling pangs of guilt about how you should have known the person was sick, or spent more time with a dying loved one, stop for a moment and think about whether those things about which you are feeling guilty are things that were actually in your control, and if they were not, then I suggest you adjust your perspective by talking to a trusted friend or seeking some type of counselling. Dr. Wayne Dyer says, *"Change the way you look at things and the things you look at change."*

- **Get Help.** When you feel that your guilt is interfering with your daily routine a professional therapist may be able to help you discover the source of these feelings. Local mental health agencies, a minister or a doctor are all good places to obtain a referral. Choose a therapist with whom you feel comfortable and with whom you have a good rapport; do not be afraid to 'shop around' for just the right fit.

Don't punish yourself with imaginary crimes such as disappointing your parents, marrying 'wrong,' exceeding the accomplishments of others or stealing parental love from siblings. The one REAL crime is punishing yourself with guilt.

Drs. Lewis Engel and Tom Ferguson, 1991

This quote illustrates the unnecessary, yet all too often guilt you may inflict upon yourself over so many aspects in your life. I would also add that it is important not to punish yourself for not having done enough for your departed loved one – a common area of blame and guilt after a death. One such client, Barbara, shared with me how she did not feel she had been patient enough while her husband was terminally ill. Upon reflection she said, *"I don't like to think about the past now, not because of how much I miss my husband but because it reminds me about how I reacted while he was ill and I don't like who I was."*

Keep in mind that you are not alone in your guilt; it is one of the most common feelings expressed in counselling sessions. I have supported a number of clients while they seek ways to come to terms with their guilt, as it can be heard and felt in so many ways:

The father whose son committed suicide says, "I'm a failure as a father."

OR the wife whose husband took his life says, "I should have seen it coming."

OR the mother whose baby died during delivery says, "I should have known something was wrong; I'm his mother."

OR the sibling whose brother committed suicide after he hadn't answered his call says, "If only I had picked up the phone."

OR the young man who left the bar early whose friend was struck by a car later that evening says, "If only I had stayed with him."

OR the 97-year-old grandfather who survived a hit and run when his grandson didn't says, "It was my time to die, not his."

OR the endless number of parents who bury children and say, "I wanted to jump into the grave right after them" AND "It should have been me."

OR the spouse who find themselves walking into an empty house, often utters, "I can't stand the silence."

OR the family member who changes the voice mail, Facebook profile picture or anything that contains a photo, or the name of the deceased.

OR the person who was not with his or her loved one at the moment of death.

OR the spouse who ponders, "What should I do with my wedding ring"?

OR the child who didn't expect to feel the loss this deeply says, "I should be in control of my emotions; I should be over it by now."

To everyone who has spent so much time second guessing and feeling the guilt of 'I should have' and 'I could have' and 'if I only', I say to you that not everything happens for a reason! You must let go of this guilt and self-blame.

Shit Happens

Although I do not believe that everything happens for a reason, I have always been the type of person who analyzes everything from every angle. I think if I understand the "why" of a situation then maybe I will be able to accept the "what" of a situation. Bad things defy logic and reasonable explanation, and are devoid of rhyme or reason; they happen simply *because*. No matter how much we search for an answer, for an explanation, or for the rationale, there does not seem to be one.

When there does not seem to be a clear explanation behind a tragedy, a loss or a death, you often rationalize in an effort to justify it so that you can feel better and start to accept what has happened. Maybe that's why so many of us live in denial; because it is just too painful, just too difficult not to have a clear reason as to why something has happened. You want and need to believe there is a bigger picture. This provides hope and comfort; the thought that a bad thing can just happen gives you the sense that you can't control your life and this is, indeed, a very scary thought.

Perhaps all you really need is to be a little bit more realistic. At Alcoholics Anonymous, the members recite a serenity prayer at the beginning of each meeting. *"God, grant me the serenity to accept the things I cannot change, the courage to change the things I can, and the wisdom to know the difference" (Reinhold Niebuhr).* This prayer reinforces the idea that some things are **in** our control, while other things are **indirectly** in our control and yet others are completely **out** of our control.

If you understand and accept this concept then you no longer need to spend your time and energy searching for "the reason"; instead, you can focus your time and energy on what you choose to do about it!

Life is 10% what happens to us and 90% how we choose to handle it.

Lou Holtz

At this juncture, I hope that you have a clearer understanding of the grief process, and the many feelings associated with it, including guilt. That being said, it's time to explore what you need in order to cope with your loss.

Maybe there's more we all could have done, but we just have to let the guilt remind us to do better next time.

Veronica Roth, 2012

CHAPTER FIVE

WHAT DO MOURNERS REALLY NEED

This is a good question. Truth be told, more often than not you really don't know what you need. You do, however, know what you don't need, but most people have been socialized not to tell others what they want. Even if you could pinpoint your actual feelings, the whirlwind of emotions you are experiencing at this time makes it pretty hard to articulate your feelings.

Peggy, whose twenty-three year old son had died in a tragic accident, was told by her mother, of all people, "At least you don't have to worry about where he is now." What does one say to something like that? Is there an answer? Clearly, one of the things you don't need is to be told how you feel.

1. You need to be acknowledged and be given permission to grieve.

Stop apologizing for crying. Contrary to what you were raised to believe, crying is not a sign of weakness. Grief is like an onion; it has many layers. The closer you get to the centre, the stronger the feeling, the more you cry. Your tears are a sign of your love for the person who has died. Most mourners apologize for crying and desperately try to hold back their tears. Why apologize? You are crying because you are hurting and if others are uncomfortable with that, then surround yourself with people who are not. Do not apologize for not crying either. Grief can be felt deeply without any outward display of sorrow. As previously stated, different cultures grieve differently; certainly Eastern and Western cultures practise different traditions of grief and mourning.

> *Grief is the last act of love we have to give to those we loved. Where there is deep grief, there was great love.*

> Zig Ziglar

2. You need people to just be there.

You need people to be present in your life – physically and emotionally. Yes, death, mourning, loss and grief are all very uncomfortable. You need to surround yourself with friends who understand that they must put their feelings aside and be there for you. It's not about them; it's about helping you in your time of need. You needn't be afraid to ask people for what it is you need. I know it would be ideal if people instinctively knew what would be helpful, but they don't. This is not the time to be humble. Very few people read minds, so if you need something, it is better to ask. Ask your friends and your family to be with you. Help them understand that avoiding you because they don't know how to help can send the message that they just don't care.

3. You need to understand that you are not the same person you once were.

Perhaps one of the greatest frustrations shared with me by my clients is that they want to feel 'normal' again. It would be dishonest of me if I did not point out that you are not, nor will you ever be the same as before. Just pause for an instant and take a moment to reflect on that. It can be an overwhelming reality. All you want is to be or feel the same; however, how can you possibly be the *same*? This harsh reality becomes part of the secondary losses I will discuss in Chapter Ten. Know that even though you will not be the same, you will still be YOU – just with a different perspective on life and death.

4. You need to understand that people are well intentioned when they say, "I know how you feel," even though it can feel so hurtful.

Of course no one else really knows how you feel. How could they? Losing a spouse, a grandparent, an aunt, an uncle, a child, a sibling, or a puppy are all entirely different experiences. Even if someone has gone through his or her *own loss,* the myriad of emotions created by this fingerprint experience dictates that it is yours and yours alone. This is also true of non-death losses such as divorce, loss of career, a move from one country to another and/or a life cycle transition (as will be discussed in Chapter Nine). People say, "I know how you feel" in an effort to connect and be supportive.

5. You need to recognize that grief is not a race.

I have often been asked the question, "How long will I feel this way?" My response as previously mentioned, remains the same, "It's not the amount of time you spend grieving; it's what you *do* with the time." Friends and family members need to respect that; it might be time to reevaluate the friendships and relationships with those who do not respect this concept. Surround yourself with the people you feel are supporting the grieving process rather than trying to push you to "get over it." Because we are all so unique, our time frame and how quickly we move back into the routines of daily life will vary. Furthermore, as will be discussed in Chapter Seven, there are a number of different factors related to the grief process such as relationship to the deceased, manner of death, previous experience with death, your own coping mechanisms, family dynamics, etc. that will directly contribute to how you process the loss.

6. You need to feel comfortable showing your true colours.

Another common challenge I hear from mourners is how difficult it is to go out in public after their loved one has died. They fear people will come up to them and ask them questions they are not ready to answer. They are concerned they will start to cry or possibly lose control. Even though you may wish you could stay inside forever, you also know how unrealistic that is. At some point you will indeed gather all the courage you can muster and venture outside the safety of your home. I supported one mother through the grief process who expressed a similar fear resulting in a completely different experience. I recall her telling me that her first trip out of the house was horrible. *"What happened?"* I asked. *"No one talked to me; it was as if I didn't exist."* People who are uncomfortable may avoid you. This can certainly be hurtful. Keep in mind, people are uncertain as to how to respond and what to say (which is no excuse) and, as such, may very well avoid you and your grief altogether. That being said, it is important that you not avoid being your authentic self, even if it makes others uncomfortable. There is no shame in grief.

7. You need to be able to talk about your grief.

Despite people's discomfort with talking about the deceased, there may be nothing more comforting to you than hearing a memory or reading a happy story about your loved one. Others may need your encouragement in order to share; they might not automatically do it, but if you ask or let others know you welcome this, you won't be sorry. These are words, thoughts and feelings that you might not have ever otherwise heard. Keep in mind; it's up to you to guide others in how to comfort you because of the common fear of saying or doing the wrong thing.

8. You need, no, you deserve to be happy.

In Chapter Four I discussed the "should" factor. At this stage I simply wish to point out that you deserve happiness, and while you may feel others are judging your demeanour or comportment, it is very important to do whatever makes you happy (as long as it's not harmful to yourself or someone else). You are responsible for your own happiness, so it's up to you to find the things that interest you and this includes anything from getting your hair or nails done to taking a course or joining a gym. You may find it difficult to motivate yourself at first. But remember, nothing changes until something changes!

9. You need to acknowledge that you are not the only one grieving.

Any one death does not only affect a single person. There are usually a number of people involved in any given loss. Everyone has his or her own relationship and history with the deceased and it is that relationship that needs to be acknowledged and processed. While you find yourself struggling with your grief, keep in mind siblings, treasured cousins, in-laws, and close friends; losing a loved one can affect the lives and hearts of a number of people.

10. You need to know that mood swings are okay.

There will be days that you seem to be coasting and then BOOM, your loss hits you again like a ton of bricks, or something triggers a memory and you get frustrated and just can't seem to get a hold of yourself. Grief can be messy, uncomfortable and confusing.

Jasmine had experienced two miscarriages and was then fortunate to have two healthy children. Upon conceiving a fifth time she miscarried again and was having a difficult time coming to terms with this third miscarriage. After a lengthy discussion, she realized that she was punishing herself for feeling low, believing she should be "over it". When I supported her permission to grieve again this lifted a huge weight off of her shoulders and in her own words, she could exhale. It's okay not to be okay.

There is no one prescribed way to feel at any given time. Grief can feel like an uninvited guest that moves in at its own pace and comes and goes as it pleases.

11. You need to follow your own spiritual path.

Religion and spirituality are intensely personal. Religion can be deeply comforting and if you have a religious framework in which to function then so much the better. Spirituality is equally comforting to anyone who regularly practises it. It is essential that you seek what is right for you without the imposition of others' opinions, beliefs or values. I had a client tell me that she desperately needed to go to the cemetery, however, in her religion one was not supposed to do so before thirty days had been observed after the burial. My suggestion was to simply do what she needed to do, as there is no right way to grieve. The right way is the way you feel in your heart.

12. You need to fake it until you make it.

If staying at home in bed was going to help bring your loved one back, I could understand doing it. Unfortunately, it cannot. I know there are hours, days and maybe even weeks when all you want to do is curl up in a ball under the covers. But what purpose will that ultimately serve? Sometimes we need to force ourselves to go out and "put on a happy face." Ironically, in doing so, you may find that you actually end up feeling some relief.

13. You need to use the words death and dying.

As I mentioned at the beginning of Chapter One, we live in a death-denying society. We don't even like to use the words death and dying. Read the obituaries; they are filled with euphemisms. You read over and over again, "It is with great sadness that we announce the passing of..." In the birth section we publicize on what date a person was born. It is very clear; we do not need to use euphemisms for birth. Yet both birth and death are natural life cycle events. If you can't say the word death or died how can you begin the process of accepting what actually happened?

14. You need to know that you are not alone in your grief; everyone has a story.

When something bad happens you begin to think, "Why me?" It is hard for you to see the bigger picture because you are so focused on what you are going through during this event. Try and remember that **no one** is immune to tragedy. When you look out the window and see people laughing, seemingly carefree, consider that they too may be struggling with some concern or tragedy. You just don't know their story... yet. Having said that, crisis brings out the best and the worst in people. I have witnessed family feuds over who loved the deceased the most, who took better care of whom, and who was the better daughter/son/mother/father. Mourning is not a contest.

15. You need to talk about your loved one.

It's important to talk about the person who died. I know I make it sound so simple, but at the same time I do recognize and acknowledge how tough this can be. Some people have a great deal of difficulty looking at a photo, let alone actually talking about their loved one. How do you talk about someone in the past tense? How do you sum up a whole relationship in a handful of anecdotes? How do you say your loved one's name without faltering or choking up? If you can't do it, then I suggest you explore why it's so difficult. Talking about your loved one and sharing special memories may be painful, yet so important to your grieving process. It's what helps keep the person's memory alive; memories are pictures we take with our heart. So even if it's difficult, it's worth it.

16. You need to recognize that time is your friend.

It has been said,

> *The clock is running. Make the most of today. Time waits for no man. Yesterday is history. Tomorrow is a mystery. Today is a gift. That's why it is called the present.*

> Alice Morse Earle

While you are going through the grieving process you may feel as though time is standing still. You may also find it hard to believe that you will ever feel normal again. Think back to the day of the funeral. Did you think you would make it through that day? Yet you did (with or without lots of tears). So again, it is not really about how long it takes; it's about what you do with the time.

The Hardest Part

When I ask mourners about the hardest part of losing someone they love, I hear a variety of responses, among them:

- Learning to live alone and the quiet in the house
- The loneliness
- Cooking for one
- Looking at old pictures
- Other people's judgement

44

- Not wanting to be a burden on my children

- Not wanting to move out of the home of a surviving parent

- What to do with the wedding ring

- Not hearing someone say, "I love you"

- Music – *"I can't listen to music because my husband was a musician and music was his language."*

The list is endless. Take a moment and think about what has been or continues to be the hardest part for you. It may be one thing; it may feel like everything. Keep in mind that ***the hardest part of losing someone you love is learning to live without that person.*** Read that sentence again, please. Once you absorb that reality, all the other challenges you encounter may become less overwhelming in relation.

Letting Go

For some, letting go is the hardest part. One of the most common challenges that arises is the question of what to do with the physical items that belonged to the deceased. This task can even become paralyzing to some. From a spiritual perspective, letting go of physical stuff is tantamount to letting go of emotional stuff from your life. In truth, clearing clutter is never just about the stuff; it addresses other issues at play beneath the surface (adapted from Sacred Space, 2005).

There seems to be tremendous guilt associated with giving away clothing. My suggestion is that if you are not ready to give it away, then *don't*. There is no rush and there is no rule that says one must rid oneself of a loved one's things, particularly right away. Families have reported deep regret after having done this too hastily.

Cathy was in her late 20's when her husband Stan died of

complications unrelated to his surgery. She was very concerned about what she should do with her husband's belongings. I suggested that if she was not ready to let them go then not to stress about it and that she would find the right time. I proposed that perhaps around the one-year mark she might take this step. Time passed and then, at a session close to the one-year anniversary of her husband's death, she seemed agitated. When I asked her what was wrong, she told me that she was feeling apprehensive, because she still didn't feel ready to donate her husband's clothes. I simply replied, "So don't. Clearly the clothes still have a very significant meaning to you, and perhaps giving them away represents another disconnection from your partner. When you recognize that the clothes do not define your loved one and that getting rid of them is not getting rid of your partner you will be able to let go of them." Approximately three weeks later she called. "Guess what, I donated the clothes."

In order to begin the process of letting go, ask yourself this: What am I holding on to and what does this achieve? Does it give you a sense of control? Or are you afraid that letting go means that you will forget or that you no longer care? Letting go **does not** necessarily mean that you are 'okay', but rather that you have started to make peace with your loss, and that you have given yourself permission to begin the process of moving forward.

The reality is, even though you cannot change whatever happened you can change how you think, feel and react. Ultimately, you need to let go of the past in order to make room for the future... and what better time to do that than in the present!

Sometimes the hardest part isn't letting go but rather learning to start over.

Nicole Sobon

Moving Forward

> *Moments we waste in sadness, anger and worries*
> *are actually moments we steal from ourselves. Life*
> *is too short, so smile and be thankful.*

Julia Turner, 2014

Over the past several years I have had the privilege of facilitating a number of support groups. Below is a list of suggestions about how the clients I have worked with have found different ways to move forward:

- Ask for help/ let friends help

- Allow yourself to do the grief work

- Seek information

- Avoid making "hasty" decisions

- Take care of yourself physically

- Remember that good nutrition is important

- Keep a journal

- Read

- Join a book club

- Make daily affirmations (These need not be spiritual or religious. Choose affirmations which reflect goals, objectives or positive thoughts in keeping with your own values.)

- Get involved in activities – social and leisure

- Volunteer. Focus on other people and not just yourself. When you find a sense of purpose, helping others helps you

- Plan new interests and things to look forward to

- Do something for someone else

- Hold onto HOPE

- Put BALANCE back into your life: pray, rest, work and play

- Laugh

- Join a grief support group – or seek the support that is right for you

- Go to church, synagogue or your religious institution

- Try saying "Yes" more often

Finding what works best can come in many forms.

Rena claims that after the death of her husband she learned to speak out. After her loss she was filled with anger for not having spoken up when she witnessed the poor treatment her husband had received at the long-term care facility he was placed in during his illness. Additionally, she was overcome with guilt believing that her husband would have advocated on her behalf if the roles had been reversed. After her husband died she went to the local newspaper and told her story, their story, in an effort to help others who might otherwise not have the courage or strength to speak out and to help prevent patient mistreatment. This action served to help Rena feel empowered and more in control of her life moving forward.

CHAPTER SIX

PRACTICALLY SPEAKING

As Stroebe and Schut (1995) describe, the grief process comprises two challenges, the emotional strain that takes place when someone you love dies and the abundance of practical decisions that need to be addressed. Questions related to wills, inheritances, bank accounts, car leases, payments, mortgages, taxes and a number of other household expenses all need attending to and are usually time sensitive. What is the difference between a death certificate and a burial certificate and how do you obtain these? Which branches of governments do you have to contact to acquire these certificates and what forms do you need to file? Are there any government subsidies available and if so, how do you apply for them?

Add to this your vulnerable emotional state and you may find yourself feeling overwhelmed!

What do you do first? To whom do you talk?

Slow down, take a deep breath and read on...

A comprehensive list of items to consider is listed below. While every province and/or state has its own laws that pertain to these items, knowing what needs to be dealt with is the first step in dealing with some very practical aspects associated with the death of a loved one.

Locate the following documents and policies:

- Private or group medical insurance policies
- Birth certificate
- Marriage certificate
- Will (may require a will search which can be done with the assistance of a lawyer or a notary)
- Life insurance policy
- Investments, stocks, bonds & certificates
- Income tax returns
- Real estate property title & deeds
- Loan/mortgage documents

Cancel the following:

- Driver's license, car registration & insurance
- Social insurance card
- Credit cards (transfer air miles, look for credit card insurance)
- Government benefits
- Leases where applicable
- Association/club memberships/subscriptions
- Nexus card
- Medicare or OHIP card, which must be returned to the government (this may have already been sent from the hospital or funeral home.)

- Passport

Other collateral items to consider:

- Transfer of services: You will also need to transfer the billing contact for utilities and other services (e.g. cell phone, electricity & heating, insurance, telephone, alarm system, etc.).

- Banking: You should also check the contents of safety deposit boxes and bank accounts. In fact, it would be wise to do this as soon as you are able since in some jurisdictions the government freezes the assets of the deceased until the estate is settled.

- A note about the passport: A valid passport should be returned by mail to the issuing country for cancellation. Include an official copy of the death certificate and a letter indicating if the cancelled passport should be destroyed or returned to you.

Apply for the following documents:

- Death certificate
- Private pension and supplemental income*
- A change of address notification from the post office if the deceased did not live at your address. This will require proof of death and a copy of the will.

*Additional benefits and supplemental income include:

- Foreign Pensions
- Private Pension plans
- War Veterans allowance
- Union Benefits

- Worker's compensation benefits from other cities

- Compensation from the city or appropriate jurisdiction (if the death was a result of a traffic accident)

Remember to:

- Dispose of all medications/syringes, etc. (at pharmacy)

- Safeguard any valuables

While this list is by no means exhaustive, it is an important start to working toward taking care of the very practical, albeit daunting, realities associated with the death of a loved one.

An important resource available is your local funeral home. The directors are equipped with knowledge and information that can help. This support begins with the funeral arrangements and can include many other practical aspects related to dealing with the death of a loved one.

I recognize that this is not an easy process, especially when the deceased has accumulated a lifetime full of memories and belongings.

Upon selling her mother's home, Veronica was both relieved and terrified about how to proceed with cleaning out the contents collected over the years. Her initial response was to get angry when anyone suggested how and where to start this process. After much discussion, Veronica realized that it wasn't actually the how and where that upset her, it was the harsh reality that she had to do this task at all. My suggestion was to seek the support of people whom she trusted and empty one room at a time, keeping things that she felt were most representative of her mom. If that meant holding onto more than less, that was okay; paring down could always be done later, however, she would never be able to get it back once it was gone.

CHAPTER SEVEN

COMFORTING THE MOURNER, OR,
A CHAPTER FOR YOUR FRIENDS

Acknowledge my grief; don't ignore me.

Author unknown

Sometimes you want to talk about your loved one, your friend or whatever loss you have sustained, but you feel uncomfortable. At the same time, people around you deliberately don't mention his or her name, thinking that this will make it easier for you. This is known as "The Elephant in the Room" and is best described in the following poem:

There's an elephant in the room.
It is large and squatting, so it is hard to get around it.
Yet we squeeze by with "How are you?" and "I'm fine"
And a thousand other forms of trivial chatter.
We talk about the weather.
We talk about work.
We talk about everything else-except the elephant in the room.

There's an elephant in the room.
We all know it is there.
We are thinking about the elephant as we talk
together.
It is constantly on our minds.
For, you see, it is a very big elephant.
It has hurt us all.
But we do not talk about the elephant in the room.
Oh, please, say her name.
Oh, please, say "Barbara" again.
Oh, please, let's talk about the elephant in the room.
For if we talk about her death,
Perhaps we can talk about her life.
Can I say "Barbara" to you and not have you look
away?
For if I cannot, then you are leaving me
Alone. . .In a room. . .
With an elephant.

Terry Kettering, 1989

I wish a copy of this poem were posted in every household, to serve as a reminder of what not to do when a death occurs. Countless clients have shared their pain over the fact that no one wants to talk about their loved one. So someone you know dies, and you find yourself instantly confronted with a plethora of emotions; you are sad, shocked, angry, confused and your friends don't know how to help. This is the chapter that you can hand over to them so that you can help them help you. Trust me, they'll thank you for it!

How Friends Can Support the Bereaved

You want to help the surviving family members; you are desperate to support them through this tragedy, yet you feel utterly and completely helpless, paralyzed by the knowledge that you cannot fix this. The question then becomes ***what do I do now?***

To begin with, it is important to recognize that everyone's

grief will appear unique and different and that a mourner's reaction to grief will depend on a number of factors (Worden, 2008):

1. Their relationship to the deceased: how close the ties, the age of the deceased, etc.

2. The manner of death: a sudden death has far different implications and challenges to the mourner than had he or she been acting in the role of caregiver to someone through a long-term illness.

3. Their own family history related to loss: the mourner's inherent coping skills and his or her familial, cultural and religious views toward death and dying.

4. The griever's support system: whom else they have in their life and what kind of network of friends, family and community is available to them. If this is an older mourner and there are not many family and friends, there might still be excellent community support. If there are limited social services, is there another system in place for bereavement counselling?

Suggested ways to comfort the mourner:

- **Allow for ALL expressions of feelings and emotions**. From laughter to crying and anger to guilt, emotions can change on a dime, so be tolerant; grieving is hard work and can be emotionally and physically draining. By offering space and time for the mourner to share his or her feelings, you are creating an environment conducive for the grief process to take place.

- **Identify the support systems available to the bereaved person/family**. If the family is not close, then identify other people – trusted friends, colleagues or a mental health professional – who can help the mourner feel connected and cared for. Karen, a client whose sister died in a car accident, used to refer to those people as "feel good people".

- **Respect religious beliefs**. Death has a way of making people turn toward or away from their religion; regardless of your own personal beliefs, it is important to respect the needs of the mourner by supporting his or her desire to become connected, stay connected, or even disconnect from religious institutions or ritual.

- **Recognize "secondary losses"**. When a loved one dies, the mourners do not just lose the person, they also lose the role of spouse or parent or child or friend and/or caretaker and all the responsibilities associated with that role (nurse, chauffeur, cook, companion, etc.). This makes for a very confusing time and an understanding of this new reality is greatly needed to help the mourner(s) reorient.

- **Follow the mourner's lead.** Encourage the bereaved to tell his or her story and share memories – good and bad, happy and difficult. Some people are not comfortable listening to the story of loss. Others have a morbid curiosity and are interested in the story for the wrong reasons. If you are someone who feels that you can actively listen without judgement, please encourage the mourner to speak freely; you will be providing him or her with an invaluable gift. Conversely, respect the mourner's wish not to talk about the loss.

- **Listen, but know your limits.** Mourners need people who can listen. If you can't, recognize this about yourself. It's okay; not everyone is wired to be an active listener. There are other valuable ways to be there for the mourner and your genuine help and concern will always be appreciated. Mark Twain said, "If we were meant to talk more than listen we would have two mouths and one ear." The simple act of listening can provide tremendous comfort to the mourner. As a friend or supporter of a mourner, you don't have to have all the answers. I often say, "I don't have the answers. I don't know what you should do. I'm not you." More often than not mourners aren't looking for answers. They simply need to be heard and know that they are not alone.

- **Don't overreact/underreact.** A mourner's reality can be overwhelming and heart wrenching, to say the least. Keep your emotions in check; mourners watch for signs of judgement. If you react in an overly dramatic manner or minimize their experience, it sends a very strong message about their grief. They need support, not judgement.

- **Recognize "triggers".** Keep in mind that dates, anniversaries, even a song, certain foods or a television show – anything that might remind the mourner of the deceased – need to be acknowledged. Mentioning, "Mother's Day is coming up; that must be difficult for you," or "I can't believe it's been a year since Bob died; how are ya doing?" can go a long way to supporting someone who has suffered a loss.

- **Identify ways to honour the deceased.** Help support ways for mourners to remember their loved one in their own way. For example, create a fund for a cause they believed in, organize a community event, construct a memory book or plant a tree. Memorial funds, candle lighting ceremonies and donations in honour of the loved one are but a few ideas.

- **Be sensitive to the external conditions of the griever's life.** This can include anything from the transition from being a couple to being a single person, the need to go to work due to financial constraints or the need to move residences and virtually start one's life over again.

- **Give permission to mourners NOT to grieve.** As previously mentioned, mourners often feel judged. If a mourner is seemingly too happy it must mean he or she wasn't really devoted to the deceased. If the bereaved is perceived as looking too sad he or she is pitied for not being able to move on. It is not for any of us to judge; mourning a loss is an entirely unique and personal experience.

- **Do concrete things.** Make a meal, run an errand or do carpool (as opposed to saying, "Call me if you need anything."). While you may mean well, mourners can be uncomfortable about asking for favours.

- **Be present in their grief.** Don't try to find something positive about the death or change the subject when the deceased's name is mentioned.

- **Remain neutral.** Do not judge feelings. When you use words such as "should or ought to" you run the risk of imposing your own perspective on their grief process.

- **Avoid catastrophizing.** Grievers will often follow the lead of others. If when close to a death or loss you become highly emotional, then perhaps it is best for you to find another way to support the family (through concrete tasks such as running errands or helping with the day-to-day needs of the family), rather than continuously breaking down in the presence of the individual or family.

- **Don't assume that time heals all wounds.**

Peggy's daughter died at the age of nine. Peggy's friends were unbelievably supportive at the time. But by year two, she was on her own. When her friends' children were graduating from elementary school, in the midst of their excitement about the upcoming graduation and dresses and parties and getting ready for high school they neglected to acknowledge that her daughter would not be a part of this milestone. It was terribly painful for Peggy. The moms and the children forgot that although they had moved on, Peggy's loss was, as always, just as real for her as ever. Being present for someone immediately following a loss is helpful; being present long term is essential.

An acknowledgment of Peggy's loss would have meant a great deal. Please be sensitive to other people's realities. As supportive as family and friends can be, an interesting phenomenon happens around the third to fourth month following the death. People start to magically disappear as if by this time the mourner should be okay and should no longer need anyone. What you need to understand is that grief has no expiry date and love, support and just checking in is always appreciated.

- **Know your resources.** It's a tremendous help to know and share what services are out there. Keep in mind that a mourner may not be ready to take advantage of a given service, but when the time comes that they are ready to avail themselves (anything from psycho-social support to a moving company) having this information or even just knowing where to find it can be invaluable.

- **Be honest.** You don't have to have all the answers. It's okay to say, "I don't know what to say." This is particularly true with children who have built-in lie detectors and will discover precisely what you are thinking just by observing your body language. Non-verbal communication sends an equally strong message to the words you are saying. Therefore, when there is a disconnect between the words you are saying and what your body is projecting, it will be evident and may create distrust in your relationship.

- **Be sensitive to the language you use.** What you say dictates how you feel about death. Don't be afraid to use the words death, dying, and deceased. That is the reality of what happened and as long as you shy away from those words, the death experience cannot be seen for what it is, a normal part of life.

While you cannot take away the pain of the loss, you can accompany the mourner(s) through the process with your understanding and support; sometimes simply **being there** is all they really need. It is important for you to understand that, *"Grief shared is grief diminished"* (Rabbi Earl Grollman).

Sometimes it is hard to know what to say to someone who is grieving and you often feel it is better just not to say anything at all. This leads to the awkward situation of not expressing to the mourner what you wish to convey and the mourner not being comforted by those close to him or her.

Following are some suggested phrases that can be helpful and some phrases which are less comforting.

Do say:

- "I'm sorry."
- "Do you feel like talking about it?"
- "How are you today?"
- "It's okay to cry."
- "I can't imagine how awful this is for you."

Don't say:

- "I know how you feel."

- "I understand."

- "You're lucky; it could have been worse."

- "It can't be that bad."

- "At least..."

- "It was G-d's will."

- "You're so strong."

- "Don't take it so hard."

Death is the one thing that connects us all. Reminds us that what's really important is who we have touched and how much we've given. Makes us realize we have to be good to one another.

Peter Petrelli, character from
the television show *Heroes*

CHAPTER EIGHT

TRIGGERS AND YOUR ATTITUDE TOWARD THEM

Whether it's conscious or not, you eventually make your decision to divide your life in half - before and after - with loss being the tight bubble in the middle. You can move around in spite of it; you can laugh and smile and carry on with your life but all it takes is one slow range of motion, a doubling over, to be fully aware of the empty space at your center.

Jodi Picoult, 2005

Triggers - those moments that remind you of your loved one – a birthday, an anniversary, family celebrations, a smell, a food, a television show... they happen all the time, every day, and some are more distinct than others. The problem with triggers is that not only are they unavoidable, they creep up on you at the strangest times and it's the unexpected ones that get to you the most. You know the ones I am talking about, the ones that you are least prepared for, like when some stranger walks into your office and tells you about someone who has just died and all the feelings, emotions and memories come flooding back to you. Sometimes those moments are like a punch in the gut – they come hard, they come fast and they are excruciatingly painful – and nothing, no pill, no amount of alcohol or drug can dull your agony. But why try to numb this feeling? Feeling pain validates the loss. You end up exhausted, depleted and then you muster up the strength to get through the moment and build yourself up again, knowing that just around the corner there might be another trigger. Yes, triggers hit you and that's pretty much it; there is no way to prevent them from happening or to predict when they might happen again. Knowing they exist helps you normalize the experience.

It should be noted that triggers aren't all negative.

During the course of my studies, in one of our classes we were asked to write the inscription we would like on our tombstones. One of my classmates responded, "SHE DID LAUNDRY WELL." No one in the class understood why she would say that, so she explained it as follows: "I had three sons, one of whom died when he was ten years old. Many years later when the two older boys grew up and went away to school, they would bring their laundry home with them." She said that for her, laundry represented a full house. It reminded her of having lots of people around, a feeling that she missed so achingly since the death of her son. For her, laundry represented a happy, boisterous household.

Triggers come in many forms. They can include, but are not limited to:

- Letters that arrive at your home addressed to the deceased
- Music
- Foods
- Television shows
- Smells

- Pictures

- Ambulances

- Fresh earth on a grave at the cemetery

- Walking on the street – disorientation – thinking you are seeing someone who looks like your loved one

- Holidays

- Birthdays

- Walking into a restaurant

Trigger statements include:

- "You could die walking across the street."

- "I'm gonna kill you."

- "I almost had a heart attack."

- "I wanted to die."

These phrases are tossed around by just about everyone at some point; the speaker never really thinks about those whose lives have been touched by these actual tragedies.

Clients have shared all sorts of memories and triggers that remind them of their loved one from feelings of jealousy when seeing other happy couples walking along holding hands, to having difficulty opening a can of soup because of the memories it conjures up of making soup for a spouse.

Shari, a woman in a widow's support group, used a great word: LAND-MINES. "It's like a land-mine; you are concentrating on something and all of a sudden, BOOM, it hits you. Hard. And you didn't even see it coming."

Another widow shared that, "Whenever I do things that we used to do together, I get sad."

Holiday Triggers – Getting Through the Holidays

Holidays can be especially tough after a loss.

June's mother died in October. When we talked about how holidays affected her, she said that the hardest day of this past year was Mother's Day. "I opened up my Facebook and saw all the postings from people honouring their mothers and my immediate thought was, f**k you all."

"Firsts" as Triggers

After a full year of experiencing every first without your loved one (holidays, birthdays, social engagements, etc.) you will not be *over it*. What you may find is that these dates and experiences may elicit a different reaction. After one calendar year, you will have gained the realization that you are capable of surviving each and every holiday, birthday and special anniversary and become empowered by this knowledge. Many happy occasions such as weddings, birthdays, and graduations take on a bittersweet feeling because while they are positive events, they will also serve as a glaring reminder that your loved one is no longer present to share in the celebration.

Melanie said that she thought the second year after her loss would be easier, however, she found that it seemed harder because if she felt sad she was angry at herself for not being stronger. She believed the hurt and pain should have been over by this point in time and was worried there was something wrong with her. I asked her when she thought she should stop counting. How would she know "enough time" had passed?

Putting pressure on yourself to move on, "suck it up" or get over it doesn't help the healing process. Don't fight it; accept it for what it is – an ending.

So here are my two cents about holidays: they can be brutal, they may hurt but they too shall pass. I know that holidays and celebrations can either mean nothing or a great deal to someone who has lost a loved one. Holidays are for celebrating, so why do you feel so sad? On these special occasions, as you look around the room and take stock of whom you have, you also become acutely aware of who is missing. So please try to stop beating yourself up because you feel so sad; instead, get together with loved ones, shed as many tears as you need to, and perhaps you will manage to recognize that, just like any other day, this day is a time not only to remember and cherish whom you have lost, but also to rejoice and appreciate what you still have. Conversely, a number of my clients have also shared their feelings of guilt if they enjoy a holiday. If you can manage to find yourself enjoying the holiday – GOOD FOR YOU!

Cognitive Triggers – When You're Alone with Your Thoughts

These are hard times. Many clients describe shower time or car rides as common times when their minds tend to wander. Realistically, this can happen any time that you might find yourself alone with your thoughts. Try to use that time to reflect on good experiences as well as sad ones. What you do or how you use alone time is a choice. What are your difficult times/places/spaces?

Behavioural Triggers Such as Avoidance

Other clients describe how they hate to go to the hospital or the funeral home because it brings back too many difficult memories. This makes sense to me. Nevertheless, I am not convinced it's the *place* that is really the issue. Granted, going anywhere that triggers sad memories of your loved one is going to be difficult. Perhaps what you are avoiding is the pain. The truth of the matter is that pain is inevitable no matter how much you try to avoid it, however, suffering is not. Do you really believe that avoiding situations and areas of discomfort will make the death easier? I am not suggesting that you must seek out these challenging places, but:

a) Is it realistic to avoid them indefinitely?

b) Will *not* going somewhere change what has happened?

Time Does Not Always Heal All Wounds

Acknowledge that the pain is a normal part of the process, and remember that you have a choice about how you can incorporate these feelings into your life. Think about it; there never seems to be a good time to say goodbye. No matter how old, how ill, how much discomfort your loved one is experiencing, there is **always** a part of you that wishes to hold on. Sure, if your loved one is in terrible pain you certainly do not want him or her to suffer. But truthfully, no one is ever ready to let go... for the longer they live, the longer you had to love them. Therefore it's important that you don't get caught up in someone else's definition of time; allow yourself to be your own time keeper.

The comments people make and the words that they use can also act as triggers.

The Umbrella of Care

In my practice, as I support clients through their grief, I often use the term "the umbrella of care" which refers to a metaphorical large umbrella that covers other people's well-meaning statements. In reality, they just don't get it. The intention is to support, to help, to make it better, but they just don't know how to do it. Just because someone is close to you doesn't guarantee that they will do and say things that are always supportive.

Handling the "Jaw Dropping" Questions

As you begin to incorporate your experience into daily life and return to your daily routines – work, parenting, social activities – you will encounter people along the way who may or may not know about your loss. It is precisely during these encounters that you will come face to face with questions that, although they come from a place of care, might leave you stuck as you search for a way to respond. While most of these questions are innocuous enough and would seem harmless under normal circumstances, they can be challenging and even excruciating to anyone who has experienced a loss, especially a recent one.

1. How ya doing?

Clients often have a tough time answering this question. For many, this question is a balancing act; while they don't feel okay, and many can't even imagine a time when they will feel okay, they also do not want to wear their hearts on their sleeves all the time. Most do not wish to be looked upon with pity. Therefore they learn to develop stock responses such as "I'm fine" or "Taking one day at a time" as a way to answer without really offering too much detail. Keep in mind who is asking the question and whether they are ready to hear the answer and that will guide your response.

2. How many children/how many siblings do you have?

This question never seems to get easier for some. Your response is simply not one that slides off the tongue. Personally, it took me a long time to find a comfortable way to answer this question; it was a number of years before I could respond, *"I had a brother who died,"* knowing only too well what would inevitably ensue after that response. The irony is that when you tell someone about the loss they become uncomfortable and then you find yourself comforting *them*. How bizarre is that? In this instance again, it is truly up to you how to respond to the question and how much information you are ready to share.

3. So how is so-and-so (referring to the deceased) doing? (posed by the person who does not know about the death)

It is always difficult to have to break this information to someone who doesn't know. There will be those people who will follow up with what can be interpreted as the inevitable insensitive question about the circumstances of the death. Again, share only what you feel comfortable sharing and with whom you feel comfortable sharing. You owe no one any explanations – even if they ask!

4. What happened?

Some people have a sense of morbid curiosity and as such will ask about every detail. It is entirely up to you as to whether you wish to respond to that question and how much detail you are comfortable providing. The question takes on an added dimension when the death is a result of a suicide. While this is an entire topic unto itself, I would be remiss if I did not mention this issue at all. Undoubtedly, it becomes particularly difficult for those of you who have experienced the death of a loved one by suicide primarily because of the strong reaction it elicits in others. It is not uncommon to say that a loved one died as a result of mental illness, medication mix up or heart attack, while others may be more upfront and honest by saying, "He or she decided to take his or her own life." How much or how little information you wish to share is a personal decision. Having said that, I do strongly suggest that you be honest with your immediate family members because:

a) Whom would you prefer that they hear it from?

b) Your challenge ahead is a tough one. Do you really want to start it off with a lie?

Ultimately, there are no easy answers to any of the above questions. Your answers may even change as time passes and you begin to integrate the loss of your loved one into your life in a different way. Trust that you will seek and develop your own comfort level, and as long as you are comfortable with the response you give then that response *is* the right answer.

> *Day to day can feel like we are walking through a minefield of memories and we don't know which ones will set off our emotions.*

> Author Unknown

An essential factor contributing to the manner in which you react and respond to triggers and the questions that are posed to you is largely dependent on your attitude.

My point is that you can't compare grief. Your pain is your pain, and my pain is my pain. Therefore, I am not trying to compare losses. I am merely trying to emphasize that no one else has the right to define what your loss means to you.

A Little Attitude Goes a Long Way

Do you remember the story of "The Little Engine that Could"? It was about a little train that didn't think it could make it up a hill, but through determination and sheer will (*"I think I can, I think I can"*) succeeded in making it all the way up the steep hill.

- Do you let negative thoughts hold you back from trying or doing something?

- Do you believe that most things don't go your way?

- Do you find yourself saying "why me"?

- Do you let daily events get to you and affect how you think or feel?

71

If you answered yes to one or more of these questions, don't despair. You are in good company; many people see the world as you do. That is to say, they feel the way they do because of the events happening around them and their lack of control over it. However, despite all this, the events themselves do not have the power to make you feel one way or the other. You may find that hard to believe, but it's true.

So if the things that happen in your life are not what make you feel happy or sad then what is it? The answer is **YOU**. You, and *only* you, have the power to control your feelings. When we hear of news that something bad has happened or is going to happen to us, it's natural to ask "why me?" and to cultivate feelings of despair.

Triggers come and triggers go. Instead of dwelling on these triggers, try to be more optimistic and focus on positive memories from your past. When you take this approach you instantly start to feel better, instead of allowing yourself to get worked up. This is the power and control that you possess.

Therefore, it's all about how you view the situation, your attitude. And it begins with recognizing that even though there are things that are very much out of your control, how you understand, process and cope with these things is very much in your control. You have the ability within you to take charge of your life and create your own destiny. It's up to you.

How you handle every situation you encounter is strongly influenced by your attitude, so let's look at how your attitude can relate to your experience with loss.

> *The longer I live, the more I realize the impact of attitude on life. Attitude, to me, is more important than facts. It is more important than the past, than education, than money, than circumstances, than failures, than successes, than what other people think or say or do. It is more important than*

appearance, giftedness, or skill. It will make or break a company ...a church ...a home. The remarkable thing is we have a choice every day regarding the attitude we will embrace for that day. We cannot change the inevitable. The only thing we can do is play on the one string we have, and that is our attitude.

Charles Swindoll (1997)

I received the following letter from a client. She was depressed and convinced that she would fail at every endeavour she tried, including counselling. She agreed to adopt a more positive outlook on life and this was what she had to share after working together for a few months.

I was thinking this morning how for at least half of my lifetime, I was convinced that I was just the type of person who would always be depressed, down and unhappy. Even in the happy times, that black cloud was always lingering in the background. I guess I had just accepted it as part of who I am. Some people are rich, some people are talented, some people are crippled and I'm just unhappy.

This morning it occurred to me that this is the longest period that I can recall where I haven't cried, felt hopeless, exhausted and fed up. It just blows my mind that this "peace" I've found, this sense of being alive, of possibilities, of empowerment has stayed with me this long. Every day, when I realize that I'm not sad, I believe a little bit more that maybe, just maybe, this may actually last – maybe I'm not destined to live in sadness.

What I find especially empowering, is that the changes I've made, in my ways of thinking, in my behaviour, in my feelings, have been so minute – but the impact they've had has been monumental – precisely like in that movie. It didn't take me a year of socializing to stop feeling lonely, it didn't take me years of therapy to stop being such a cynic, it didn't take a miracle to gain optimism. It was small changes, baby steps, tiny moves in a better direction – and my life feels transformed.

Don't get me wrong, I'm constantly aware of the possibility that I can relapse – that I'll get lazy and fall back into old patterns. But, I'm also constantly aware that I'm capable of changing that if it happens, and that even if I'm not, there are people who can help me. My happiness doesn't come from the fact that I think that I can never be sad again, it comes from the fact that I know that if I do get sad, I can get out of it again.

Just one degree, just a tiny effort, just that extra step – can make a world of difference. That's what keeps me going.

Your attitude in life determines your altitude.

Zig Ziglar

CHAPTER NINE

NON-DEATH LOSSES

Everything you do in your life relates to loss in some form or another, whether it's professional, personal, psychological, or emotional. It all boils down to first having something and then that something being taken away from you. You are forced to adapt or adjust (for better or for worse) without that person, that object or that situation. Some of us do it with grace and poise; others never seem to quite find our place. Everyone adjusts differently; no one comes through unscathed. I can tell you, though, that after all these years of accompanying families through the death of a family member, the one thing I am absolutely certain of is that NO ONE is immune and that there is no template or guidebook for loss. When it comes right down to it, all you have to help you get through this process is you, and if you are fortunate, a good support system of friends and family members who can respect and empathize with what you are going through.

It's Not Just About Death

It was a Thursday afternoon, September 27th, at 2:30 PM. I was in a classroom at the school where I was Dean of Student Services, talking to grade six students about a fund-raising initiative that I was working on with the grade six English teacher. She had asked me if I could come into her class and explain the assignment. "You speak so well, and you understand the project better!" Naturally, feeling flattered, I agreed.

As I was finishing up the discussion the rabbi, who was Head of School, entered the class and asked to speak with me. He ushered me out of the classroom, and thinking nothing of it, I followed him out. I remember making idle chit chat; he said something about his back hurting him and I said something about stress. It's amazing, the details you remember in a situation like this.

As we reached the second floor of the school I figured we'd go to my office, as we had many times before when we met to speak. But he said he preferred to go to his office. When we got there I sat down, he shut the door, sat down and looked directly at me and said, "It's not good news; we're eliminating your position at the end of December."

It felt surreal; my world came crashing down in a heartbeat. You see, I have always defined myself very much by my work. Who I am (good, bad or indifferent) was only as good as where I worked or what I was working on, how people perceived me and even the title I held. So if I wasn't the Dean of Student Services, who was I? I'm embarrassed to admit, the fact that I am a wife, a mother, a daughter, a friend, a therapist, a teacher, and a facilitator, at that particular moment none of it seemed to matter. Someone was taking away my role, my identity without my consent. Sure, I had left jobs before, but, I loved this job. I didn't want to go and I could not wrap my head around the fact that there did not appear to be a damn thing I could do about it. This was out of my control.

What has become crystal clear is that loss encompasses EVERYTHING. So while my work has primarily focused on individuals and families who have struggled with the death of a loved one, every challenge, every problem we face can be related back to the loss of something.

The following is a list of losses you may face on a day-to-day basis that often go unrecognized, and are therefore not validated. Only when you begin to define them as losses can you begin the process of treating them in a helpful and productive way. As you review the list you may identify with some of these losses. This may serve as a starting point in order to give you insight into your feelings and reactions.

Loss of *Significant person*

Loss of *Relationship*

Loss of *Role*

Loss of *Health*

Loss of *Bodily function*

Loss of *Body image*

Loss of *Sexual functioning*

Loss of *Control*

Loss of *Freedom*

Loss of *Safety*

Loss of *Identity*

Loss of *Innocence*

Loss of *Job/Income*

Loss of *Religious beliefs*

Loss of *Home or Property*

Loss of *Treasured object*

What do you notice? I was amazed when I first saw the list. My first thought was, "I'm a loser." I found it helpful to re-examine these as losses primarily because how you grieve doesn't necessarily change based on the significance of the loss. Today my private practice encompasses identifying experiences of non-death losses and working through them as part of the healing process.

The author Isabel Allende once wrote, *"I never said I wanted a 'happy' life but an interesting one. From separation and loss, I have learned a lot. I have become strong and resilient, as is the case of almost every human being exposed to life and to the world. We don't even know how strong we are until we are forced to bring that hidden strength forward."*

Other Forms of Loss

There are some forms of loss that are not final. There is no mourning period, no ritual, but there is ongoing grief.

When I was speaking with a colleague whose husband had survived a severe stroke, she shared a little bit of what her family's loss looked and felt like. Her words were very poignant; she described that while her adult children loved and respected their father, it seemed they had already made their peace and said goodbye. Their father was there, but not really there anymore.

Only others who have experienced this reality can possibly understand what it is like to relive this type of loss every day. This scenario is true for families of individuals with mental illness, Alzheimer's, dementia and a host of progressive illnesses or debilitating conditions. Suddenly, your relationship with a life partner has changed and, with the loss of intimacy, the life you were meant to have has been snatched away and a host of responsibilities thrust upon you.

As caregiver, you are not able to focus on much else in life – the good and the bad – from the joy of children and grandchildren to the proper mourning of the spouse who is alive but not the same person you married. When someone dies there is a funeral, a mourning period and recognition that there has been an end. Unfortunately, when you, as caregiver, are faced with a loved one who is experiencing a change in cognitive capabilities, mental health issues or Alzheimer's, you may not always immediately acknowledge it as a loss. Furthermore, others may forget or even ignore you and your loved one because being around you makes them really uncomfortable. In turn you are often left alone with minimal support or understanding. It is therefore incumbent upon you to recognize the situation for what it is – a loss – and give yourself permission to grieve accordingly.

Life certainly doesn't always offer you what you expected; nevertheless, you do have choices about how you react.

So what can you do?

- Begin by acknowledging the non-death loss or change in your life as a loss.

- Seek help and support from friends and outside services such as a mental health professional, support group and/or local social service centre.

- Empower yourself. Educate yourself with as much information as possible about the illness or change of life circumstance. The hospital, doctor or local library can offer such information.

- Be patient with yourself. Know that there will be days and times that prove more difficult than others so don't be afraid to ask for help if you feel you need it.

At the end of the day, Norman Cousins says it very well:

Death is not the greatest loss in life. The greatest loss is what dies inside us while we live.

CHAPTER TEN

SECONDARY LOSSES

Anyone who has lost something they thought was theirs forever finally comes to realize that nothing really belongs to them.

Paulo Coelho, 2005

There is a forgotten aspect of loss; not only do you lose your loved one, your friend, your pet, your profession, your home, your relationship, you also lose parts of yourself that went along with any of the aforementioned. These are commonly referred to as secondary losses. They are aspects of your role, your identity, your status, your financial situation and your sense of self – the person formally known as "you". If these losses are left unrecognized, you can find yourself out of sorts without really understanding why.

I work with a number of people who, in general, come to me for counselling feeling 'lost' or 'displaced'. For example, when someone in their life has died, it has been my experience that they often experience a secondary loss – most notably, their sense of purpose. It goes without saying that if you spend a significant amount of time devoted to caring for your loved one, you naturally find yourself adrift when your loved one dies. Even if one does not spend time as a caregiver or if the loss is sudden, one's role, lifestyle, and identity are altered in some way.

Some examples of secondary losses:

- Young children who lose a parent will often feel as if they have, in fact, lost both parents, as the surviving spouse becomes discombobulated and disoriented while mourning the death of his or her partner.

- The couple whose child dies loses the role of parent *even if* they have other children, since the relationship and interaction with each child is so unique.

- The brother or sister whose only sibling dies loses the role as a brother or sister and becomes an only child. I was not born an only child; I became one. Ever since my brother died, I am acutely aware that to my parents, I am all they have left. I remember shortly after my brother died, my mother uttering the words, "Two is not enough" when discussing my feelings around how many children my husband and I were planning to have. The loss of normalcy and need to be perfect can come with the pressure for a sole surviving child. I have worked with a family where they have sadly buried two children. The surviving child said to me, "I can't get ill."

- There are also instances where the relationship you ***never had*** is felt enormously. If you didn't have a close relationship with your parent, your child, or your sibling and then they die, the reality that you can never have that relationship is perceived as a secondary loss.

Riva described her secondary losses as follows: Not only did I lose my partner; because we are getting older, I have also lost my youth, my ability to do things the way I did them before.

82

The Other Side of Loss – It's Not Always Devastating

Kurt: "Our marriage was over years ago. She was a total SOB, she was abusive, but I still completely supported her. I wished her dead more times than I can count. And then she died. I don't miss her one bit. I don't feel one ounce of grief."

Me (dumbfounded): "So how can I be helpful?"

Kurt: "I feel guilty that I am not sad and that I have to pretend to be grieving for my children."

Not all loss is shattering. In some situations, the surviving family members can even feel relieved. But wait; before you begin to judge, remember that everyone has a different relationship with the deceased and sometimes that relationship died long before the person did; sometimes that relationship was troubled from the start.

Similarly, not all miscarriages are devastating, even though they may be so very difficult. It is important that the couple who experience the loss define their feelings about the miscarriage, as opposed to allowing others to define the meaning of the miscarriage for them.

What I am trying to convey is that it is all about *meaning*. I would never attempt to tell someone what meaning to attach to his or her loss. Only the people directly involved in the relationship can identify what the true feelings of loss (grief, sadness, anger, relief) are. So if you don't find yourself overwhelmed with feelings of grief, take some time to assess your relationship. What did it mean to you? You can't feel loss if you never felt you had anything to lose. Are you not grieving because of the state of the relationship or are you still numb and not yet ready to process your feelings? Do you need help discerning between the two? Perhaps you are grieving the relationship you never had. Whatever the answer is, the meaning lies in your definition.

Scratching the Surface – What's Really the Issue?

Shortly after I meet with a client, it is not unusual for me to discover that his or her loss is compounded by a number of other unresolved issues haunting him or her from the past. For example:

- A woman came to counselling three years after her parents were murdered. During the course of our session she recounted a story about how difficult it was for her to trust people. She revealed that she did not trust anyone, not even her husband. When we probed a little further, she shared with me that her husband had had an affair five years earlier and that she had never been able to forgive him. This became the focus of our sessions. As she learned how to face her relationship challenges she recognized that this was the underlying issue she had been struggling with. She had come to terms with her parents' murder. While devastating, it had actually been dealt with; the accused had been incarcerated, the funeral had helped with closure, and she had supportive and loving siblings. She had learned to let go of her anger and face her issues of trust while confronting the problems in her relationship.

- A mother whose son committed suicide was wrought with guilt about what she should have or could have done. As we explored further, I discovered that her behaviour pattern, relentlessly blaming herself for things, was a deep-seated trait that she had exhibited as far back as she could remember.

- A son spent his entire childhood being dismissed by his mother, being criticized and told that he was not good enough. Upon his mother's death, he then grieved not only for the loss of his mother but for the loss of the relationship they had never had.

- A daughter was the sole caregiver for her mother. When her mother died, not only did she mourn her death, she also lost her sense of purpose.

All this is to say that there are additional losses or other deep-rooted issues that emerge when the death of a loved one occurs. Acknowledge these secondary losses if they arise and seek the support of family, friends or a mental health professional when appropriate.

Every one of us is losing something precious to us. Lost opportunities, lost possibilities, feelings we can never get back again. That's part of what it means to be alive.

Haruki Murakami, 2005

CHAPTER ELEVEN

THE FORGOTTEN GRIEVERS – KIDS ARE GRIEVERS TOO

Having worked in the field of bereavement counselling for so many years, I have a good grasp of the importance of involving children in the grief process. This knowledge was put to the test when one day, some years ago, I found my family faced with the death of a much admired, much loved uncle.

Our uncle died after a brief illness in May of 2000. Because our family had been very close to him it was clear that we would attend the funeral with our children, eight and six years old at the time. It seemed natural, given my understanding of how children grieve and given the relationship that our girls had with their great-uncle, that they too were grieving.

My husband and I spoke with the girls about what they could expect to experience before, during and immediately following the funeral; this included describing to them as best we could what they would see, how people might react, and what the service would look like. All seemed well until I mentioned to my family that the girls would also be coming to the cemetery for the burial. This announcement was met with a great deal of anxiety and apprehension by various family members, so much so that I, myself, started to question whether it was a good idea. Nevertheless, I decided to go with my instinct, particularly since the girls had already expressed a desire and willingness to attend.

The day of the funeral arrived and we went to the funeral home where the girls were met with warm smiles. The service was beautiful and both children listened and watched as other family members eulogized our uncle. We then left for the cemetery where our younger daughter promptly made her way directly to the front of the crowd to witness the burial service and rites. As is customary in our tradition, each of the mourners is given the honour of shoveling a small amount of earth into the grave. It was at this moment that my father-in-law, whose brother was being buried, completed this task, took a step back from the grave and stood alone. My younger daughter approached her grandfather and gently held his hand. He looked down at her and lovingly kissed her on the forehead. It was then that I was able to confirm what I had instinctively and professionally known, that even at this intense moment of grief, the presence of the children served not only to comfort the mourners but also to remind them of how life goes on.

Later that same year, the father of a friend died after a brief battle with cancer. Naturally, out of respect, my husband and I attended the funeral. Our younger daughter came with us simply because we were on our way somewhere else after the service. No longer a rookie at funerals, she sat patiently during the service. As the procession was making its way to the hearse and the attendees were leaving the sanctuary, she looked up at me brightly and said, "Hurry up Mom, I don't want to miss the good part."

I retell these two vignettes to emphasize that *children are not born with a fear of death and dying*; it is we, the adults around them, who *teach them this fear and alarm.* You send strong signals when you say, "A cemetery is no place for a child," or express your fears with comments and non-verbal cues that broadcast the message that something bad or terrible happens at funerals. If you truly want to help or sensitize younger generations to support our elderly and your loved ones then you must begin by recognizing the effects of your own behaviour around death and bereavement.

Some practical suggestions:

- You need to use every opportunity to talk about life and death as part of your everyday routine. For example, when you purchase flowers, talk about how every living thing has a life – a beginning, a middle and an end; some lives are longer, others are shorter. It's important that you use the correct language when you talk about death, as opposed to euphemisms and slang words. Telling a child that someone died as a result of an accident leaves ambiguity in the mind of the child. Be specific, without being unnecessarily graphic or explicit; the word accident to many children signifies urinating in their pants.

- You need to be HONEST, SIMPLE and speak with LOVE. There is no place for sugar coating things. *"Grandma died because her heart stopped working,"* or *"Grandpa was very, very, very sick – a sick that couldn't be fixed."* Remember that children are more aware than we give them credit for. *One mother told her daughter that their cat had died. When the child asked what had happened the mother said, "It's okay honey. Your cat is now with G-d. He was such a good cat that G-d needed him." The child looked at her confused and replied, "What does G-d need a dead cat for?"*

- Physically place yourself at their eye level; it is helpful to sit with your child, place him or her on your lap or kneel down to his or her level so that you are not towering over him or her as you talk together.

- Acknowledge the developmental age of the child. While I always state that you know your children best, in general, children over the age of five can and should be involved in the funeral process. This is the age when children start to understand that death is *irreversible,* which means that unlike the videos they are all too often exposed to where a character dies and then magically comes back to life, in real life living things do not come back to life. Keep in mind that some children are more mature than others; some cannot sit through a funeral service while others can sit quietly. Guide yourself accordingly.

- Make sure there is someone your child trusts near him or her explaining what is going to happen. Ideally, this should not be one of the mourners. It could be a family friend, trusted baby sitter or other close family member.

- Don't wait for a significant death to bring your children to the funeral home or cemetery. Often the first time a child enters a funeral home or cemetery is when someone close to him or her has died. Instead, take the opportunity to bring your children to a funeral when the service is not for a close relative or friend. Or go visit a deceased relative at the cemetery on a nice day when you can explain what happens without the same emotional reaction that occurs when someone close to you or them has died.

On a personal note, one beautiful sunny day I decided to take my older daughter to the cemetery. When she asked where we were going, I said, "To the cemetery." She responded, "Cool!"

Ultimately, helping children cope when a death occurs is comprised of three basic elements:

- **Information:** Who died? How did the person die? How will this affect them?

- **Choice:** Should they attend the funeral?

- **Support:** Who is going to be there for them now? The question is simple. Children want to know that they will be taken care of, regardless of who died. They need to know whom they have left and who will take care of them.

In order to comfortably and appropriately respond to your children you also need to understand where your fears, phobias and attitudes toward death come from. You must find the appropriate people and places to express your concerns, share your thoughts and address your needs so that the next generation understands that death is simply a part of life. If you can teach this to your children, then perhaps their loved ones can truly die without every really going away.

One of the most frequently asked questions is whether or not a child should attend the funeral. My response is twofold:

1. As mentioned, you know your child best.

2. It depends. It depends on the age, on the developmental level of the child, on the temperament and disposition and on the circumstances surrounding the death of the loved one. Once all these factors have been taken into consideration, it is important that the child be given the *choice* of whether or not to attend. In order to help the child make that decision he or she would benefit from being prepared in advance about what to expect.

Other suggestions include:

- It is helpful to keep in mind that including children in some decision-making helps to send the message that they are part of the process. Do not shelter your children from tragedy; death is an inevitable part of life. Learning about death teaches us about life. Therefore, allow your child to be included in family rituals related to the death.

- Share your emotions about the loss with the children involved and encourage them to share their feelings about what has happened. Parents need to understand that children are intuitive and are quick to pick up on emotional cues, so it is important to be genuine with your emotions and coping strategies. You are their role models and as such, they will take their cues about how to express themselves from you. For example, it's okay to cry. Share with your children what the deceased meant to you. We cry because we loved someone and we are going to miss him or her. Encourage open discussion that is age appropriate. Express your own feelings clearly, while being mindful not to offer too much information. You can also encourage your child to express himself or herself through art, music or play.

- At the same time, you cannot force discussion. Let the child guide the discussion; create an environment in which he or she feels free to ask questions as often as he or she would like. Refrain from using euphemisms or clichés to describe the death such as "gone to sleep", "going on a long trip" or "lost" as children are very literal and will fear going to sleep, travelling or being lost.

- Try to maintain as much routine and stability in the child's life as possible; routine is reassuring. Some children mistakenly believe that somehow the death is their fault; it is important to reassure them that the deceased did not want to leave them.

- Seek opportunities for rituals and/or recognition of the deceased on special occasions such as birthdays, holidays, and the anniversary of the death. Honouring the memory of the person who died is a very important and meaningful way to acknowledge and respect the grieving process.

- Remember, it's okay not to have all the answers. While your children look up to you for support and guidance, certainly not having the answer to "Why did this happen?" can feel paralyzing. It is important to recognize that sometimes you cannot possibly have the answer to this question; you may be struggling with understanding what and why such a tragedy has occurred. Being honest is essential in this instance. Additionally, recognize that the question often represents an underlying fear of "Who will take care of me now?" or "Can this happen to me?" That being the case, it is best to address this fear by reassuring your child that above all else, he or she will be looked after.

- Seek support for yourself. You cannot help others if you do not help yourself first. Even on airplanes there is a reason they tell you to put the oxygen mask on yourself first; you cannot be helpful to anyone else if you are not okay. In order to best help your children you must ensure that you have the support you need; therefore, if you or your partner seem to be having difficulty coping with the death of a loved one seek professional support.

Children will follow your lead... Lead well, lead confidently and you will teach them perhaps the hardest yet most important lesson in life.

There is no destination, no arrival, no ending place in the journey of grief. There is no road map to follow, no formula, and no way to hurry the journey or bypass the pain. There are passages to live through, not stages that we move past in a lockstep, hierarchical order. To force ourselves or our children into a linear grieving "process", evaluating where we are on the ladder of grief, is a vain attempt to control and manipulate a "journey of the heart." This journey cannot be controlled; it can only be lived through by each one of us in our own time in our own way.

Barbara Coloroso, 2000

CHAPTER TWELVE

CREATING "NEW NORMALS"

We are all faced with a series of great opportunities brilliantly disguised as impossible situations.

Charles R. Swindoll

When someone you love dies you are changed forever. In my personal and professional experience, it is a fallacy to think that life will ever be the same as it was before the death of your loved one. How can it be? With the loss of your loved one, your whole world order has been changed. That doesn't mean you will never experience happiness again. Life will be different without the presence of that person. The acute feelings of loss will not be quite as intense over time, but they will never entirely disappear. The strong feelings of grief do soften over time as you begin to experience something I refer to as **'new normals'**.

These new normals come in all shapes and sizes. As I recounted in Chapter Nine, I was working in a professional position that I loved when the position was eliminated. I found myself at a loss as to what to do next. Sure, I always had some private work, but I had never been laid off before and it was very demoralizing. I didn't know how to get myself to move forward. In an effort to make a "new normal" for myself, I registered for a whole series of networking breakfasts, lunches, and cocktails; I was determined to get myself out there and to let people know who I was and what I could do. *Ready or not world, here I come.*

Well, there I was at my first outing – a woman's networking group. Normally I do not consider myself a shy person, but with the feelings of the recent lay off still raw, I guess I was feeling a little more vulnerable than I realized because by the end of the two hours, after meeting some very interesting women (and some men), hearing a highly dynamic speaker, and making some important connections I went directly to my car, climbed in and sobbed uncontrollably. What was going on? I was still in shock. I could not wrap my head around the fact that "This is where I am now. This is what my life has become. I've been reduced to selling myself?" And to add insult to injury, as the keynote speaker had so blatantly pointed out, very few of us had distinguished ourselves as very memorable or impressive in our personal introductions. So because I tend to personalize *everything* I've ever done, I got caught up in the feedback and began to feel sorry for myself, allowing myself to believe what the presenter was saying, and started to think, "She's right; I'm not special. If I was special I would have stood out; I would have had more to say." I was experiencing loss of a very different kind… loss of confidence, and a loss of self. It is so easy to get caught in this trap if you allow yourself to go there. I CHOSE not to go there, but I also learned that it's tough to adapt to new normals.

Through this experience, I learned three important lessons that can help you adapt to your new normals:

1. **Don't let others define you.** Loss leaves you vulnerable and more susceptible to personalizing all that you hear around you. It's easy to get caught up in feeling sorry for yourself and losing your confidence. Remember that no one can take away your confidence or anything else without

your permission. You are worthy and have unique gifts to share with the world; you merely have to believe in yourself. So what did I learn? Be discerning with what you listen to and/or take to heart; there are a lot of 'expert opinions' out there; however, if you trust and believe in yourself, others will too. I might have been briefly discouraged, but by checking in with myself I was able to recalibrate before long.

2. **Perception is reality.** There will be good days and there will be bad days. Grief can be like the wind, which can shift your mood depending on the day, the situation, the social setting or the task at hand. On the day of the networking meeting I found myself feeling sad, frustrated, angry, and mostly scared. I felt, "Poor me; she's right; I am never going to amount to anything," which she had not said, but which was my interpretation of her message. I *hated* the speaker for pointing out the obvious, but what she had really done was hit a nerve. The next day I woke up feeling completely different; I felt empowered, energized and self-aware knowing that I had embraced a new normal. I had made the choice to pick myself up, dust myself off and get moving. I realized the event itself hadn't been so bad after all; I had made some new connections and someone had even offered me some contract work on the spot! You see what you want to see. My perception of the situation had shifted from a negative to a positive reality.

3. **We all have *choices*.** If you want to succeed, you need to set some goals. In order not to become overwhelmed, it is best to set both short and long term goals. Success breeds success; establishing manageable, daily goals so that you experience success, however big or small, will help you stay organized and positive about both tasks and regular leisure activities. If sitting at home and indulging in self-

pity is going to achieve what it is you hope to accomplish, by all means, go ahead and do that. But if connections, work and success are what you are looking for then I suspect you need to reach out – one step at a time. How can you do this? Seek support services, organizations and networking groups in your area that may be in keeping with your goals. You need to be the starring role in your life.

Nothing changes until something changes. Personally, I work out; the gym is my happy place. Think about what makes you happy. Is it volunteering? Listening to music? Reading? Hanging out with friends? It doesn't matter what it is *"As long as it's not illegal, immoral or life-threatening"* (Barbara Coloroso, 1994). While change can be overwhelming, when you embrace it you will come to realize that you are capable of moving forward – of loving, of laughing and of living again.

It is perfectly normal to want to go back to a time when your loved one was still with you, or when your work or your life hadn't changed. It's scary when things change. You become fearful of the change. Fear can paralyze you into a fight or flight response. Try to think about fear as your default protective factor that isn't necessarily real. So rather than fight the change, recognize that the only constant in life is change so even if it is not what you are used to, it doesn't mean it will be all bad. New normals are about letting go of the life you had planned and living the life that is.

> *Ultimately it is not the grief that stops us from starting life over - But the fear of losing it all again.*
>
> Christina Rasmussen, 2013

Coping with New Normals

The human capacity to cope with adversity is phenomenal. I always believed this, however, my belief was confirmed in 2003 when I had the privilege of accompanying fifty-seven grade eleven students as the mental health professional for a special program called March of the Living. The trip revolved around touring Poland and Israel. In particular, the first week the students toured Poland, walking through sites where Nazi concentration camps once existed. Accompanying the group was a Holocaust survivor who shared his real life experiences. His participation indicated that he had made an entirely new life despite the horrors he had endured. It was this experience that highlighted for me man's ability to overcome even the worst atrocities and still have the capacity to move on. I do not know how long it will take you, or how you will accomplish it, but when you accept the changes in your life – you are taking the first step toward accepting your new normal.

After the Boston Marathon bombing on April 15, 2013, one of the psychologists interviewed on CNN spoke about three essential elements in order to help deal with loss:

1. **HOPE:** the belief that your circumstances can and will get better.

2. **FAITH:** the belief in something, either religious belief and/or a belief in a higher power and a world in which there is more good than evil.

3. **SUPPORT:** a system of family or friends with whom you have a connection so that you will never feel alone.

You CAN and you WILL find your way.

Pain means you're growing. Fear means you're risking. Tears mean it mattered. Take what hurts you and let it help you.

Mandy Hale

CHAPTER THIRTEEN

THE IMPORTANCE OF LAUGHTER

You need to laugh. Laugh out loud and laugh often.

CHAPTER THIRTEEN

THE IMPORTANCE OF LAUGHTER, REALLY

I have been blessed with a good sense of humour (thanks to my father) and, as such, jokes and laughter have always been present in my life. Therefore it seems only natural that I would incorporate this personality trait into my professional life.

In my practice, humour has become a powerful technique to help clients examine many aspects of their lives. When used appropriately, this strategy can prove extremely therapeutic. That is to say, you need to develop the ability to laugh at yourself and with yourself, as this can really help you through some of the toughest times of your life. It is humour that can provide you with a sense of control over the stress that goes along with dealing with a tragedy or battling an illness, giving you more power over your daily mood. I am in no way suggesting that humour or laughter will replace or resolve your grief or mourning. Your tears will not instantly turn to laughter. What I *am* saying is that your attitude toward death is often one of strict seriousness when, in fact, laughter can be enormously therapeutic during the grief process (adapted from the Centre for Grief Journey).

A sense of humor can help you overlook the unattractive, tolerate the unpleasant, cope with the unexpected, and smile through the unbearable.

William Novack & Moshe Waldoks, 2006

Laughter helps you sustain an upbeat, optimistic frame of mind, even on the bad days.

This more positive emotional state can help give you the resilience you need to cope with the grief you are experiencing. A good belly laugh also boosts your energy level on the days when you don't even feel like getting out of bed.

Humor and laughter provide a means of "letting go" of the anger and anxiety that build up on your worst days.

Paul E. McGhee, 2002

Laughter also reduces muscle tension. It is well known that laughter has healing qualities as proven by the research of Norman Cousins (2005) in *The Anatomy of an Illness*. He demonstrates how endorphins released by laughter help to act as an anaesthetic to both physical and emotional pain.

Life does not cease to be funny when people die any more than it ceases to be serious when people laugh.

George Bernard Shaw

Many of us tend to deal with the unknown by mocking it. There are comedians and writers who devote their careers to this subject alone. In a 1927 essay, "Der Humor", Sigmund Freud theorized that this dark humour is really the ego's refusal to be distressed by reality; in short, humour is a coping mechanism for grief and mourning. You need not feel guilty about laughing for it is not a sign that you don't care; it is merely a way to release some tension in a situation or circumstance that might otherwise be highly overwhelming. So, the next time you, or someone you know says something funny, don't be afraid to laugh. Whatever tickles your funny bone and helps release those endorphins will help you through this difficult time.

To help get you started, here are some hand-picked jokes on death that I have always found pretty funny:

- Being cremated is my last hope for a smoking hot body.

- Fun science fact: If you took all the veins in your body and laid them end-to-end... you would die.

- Before his death at 100 years of age, Bob Hope's wife asked him where he wanted to be buried. His answer, "Surprise me."

He who laughs...LASTS.

Mary Pettibone Poole, 1938

CHAPTER FOURTEEN

GONE BUT NOT FORGOTTEN

*A memory is what is left when something happens
and does not completely unhappen.*

Edward De Bono

On the twentieth anniversary date of my brother's death, I wrote the following email to my parents:

I hate today... not the day, nor the date, I hate the idea of what today represents. I hate that there has to be an anniversary, I hate that I never seem to know the right thing to say to you, I hate that I have to stress about saying the right thing to you, I hate that it happened, I hate that the two people that I love most in this world have to live with this pain, I hate that I can't make it better, I hate that I don't have another sibling to share this feeling of hate with, I hate that I have grown somewhat accustomed to being an only child, I hate that he didn't get to meet my kids, I hate that there are days that I don't think of him at all, I hate that I don't cry so much when I think of him, I hate that it's been 20 years, I hate that it's been 20 seconds... I miss him. Thinking of you today.

On December 3, 2014, twenty-six years after my brother Andy's death I wrote:

Dear Mom and Dad,

It's December 3rd, just another day, it's just another day. No it's not just another day. Ever since December 3rd 1988, no day has ever been just another day. Yet while I remember what we lost, I also choose to be grateful for what I still have... two loving parents, two healthy children, a unique and special husband and supportive friends.

Have whatever day you choose to have.

Hugs,
Corrie

Every year I search for the words that will best describe the experience of honouring the memory of my brother. I have come to terms with the fact that it is not the words we use but the feelings we convey and share that serve to preserve the relationship.

A number of clients I meet fear they will forget their loved one. No, you will not. But it is your responsibility to keep that relationship alive. My daughters never met my brother Andy, yet they know so much about him because I choose to share stories and anecdotes of who he was, so that my daughters know him and what he means to me. This is best exemplified by the words of Morrie Schwartz from *Tuesdays with Morrie* by Mitch Albom (1997):

> *As long as we can love each other and remember the love that we had, we can die without ever really going away. All the love that we shared is still there, all the memories are still there. They remain in the hearts of everyone we have touched and*

nurtured while we were alive...Death ends a life, not a relationship.

Dr. Spencer Johnson wrote the book, *The Present,* in which he advises us to *"learn from the past, plan for the future but live in the present"* (2003). If you are not already doing this, and I suspect you are not, this is the time to start trying your very best to do so. If you spend all your time focused on the past, fixated precisely on the things you cannot change or worried about the future, you lose all the time you could be focusing on today.

> *It is very difficult to make predictions, especially about the future.*
>
> Winston Churchill

Other clients shared a number of regrets about how they wished they had handled things, particularly regarding their relationship with the deceased. In my opinion, regret is a wasted emotion. It serves no purpose except, perhaps, to make you feel bad about something you cannot change. So rather than spending your time regretting things or worrying about things that have yet to happen, *learn* from the past and *plan* for the future but *live* in the NOW.

How Do We Learn?

When the fog of your initial grief lifts, here are some questions that you can ask yourself in order to help you process the experience:

- What did the person mean to you?

- What have you learned about yourself, about other people, about life from this person and this loss?

- What good has come from this difficult experience? Are there things you appreciate more?

- Who are the people who have been there for you? Were they the people from whom you expected support?

- In what ways have you grown or matured from this experience?

You may be amazed by what you learn from some of the answers. Just because the death of a loved one is a very sad time in your life, doesn't mean it has to be an all negative experience. Sounds crazy? Perhaps. When you allow yourself to truly feel the loss you may learn something rather surprising; pain is unavoidable; agony is not.

Look on every exit as being an entrance somewhere else.

Tom Stoppard, 1967

I have travelled the long journey of grief, and I am still travelling it. I have had the privilege of accompanying so many individuals and families through their journey. Together we have laughed and we have cried, we have learned and we have questioned, we have lost and we have found...but first and foremost we have grieved.

Positive Reflections

The greatest gift I have received throughout my career in counselling is the feedback from those I have been privileged enough to counsel. To all of you who have sustained a loss and shared that experience with me, I am forever grateful and eternally honoured for the trust you have bestowed upon me.

Below are some positive reflections from families that I hope will resonate with you.

Lily, who had experienced three miscarriages stated, "I love the way I feel after talking with you. I feel like I can finally exhale."

Barry said, "The good thing about my mother's death is that I had to grow up. She did everything for me. Her death forced me to become more responsible and learn to do things on my own. It's very important."

Shari expressed, "I relied on Mom for everything to a fault and now I have learned that whether I like it or not, I have to make my own decisions because she is no longer with me; my life still goes on."

Maria shared her reflections about the death of her husband. "It's also a celebration of life. I thank God for having had him in my life for so many years."

Lori, who experienced a still birth, and then a miscarriage after two successful pregnancies, wrote the following to me after a support group meeting entitled "Healing Together" at the West Island Women's Centre in Montreal, Canada:

"I felt great today - upbeat and energetic - more noticeable than in recent memory. I think last night played a big part in that. It was comforting to be there and to hopefully help someone else. I didn't want to say this last night but I'm glad Christine (another member of the group) had a son to go home to after leaving the hospital. I kept this to myself because I didn't want to minimize or make light of her pain. The silence, however, is deafening and could make everything that much more unbearable. Of course she'll never know this... thankfully.

When I listen to myself, our story, it sounds terrible and was terrible but I'm relieved and grateful that it didn't define us in a way that ruined us or didn't allow us to move forward. That's the message I would want to convey to others living a similar fate. It's complicated to want to share in someone's pain and be inspirational at the same time.

Like you, I am happy that Christine was there. Not only to share her story and address her grief, but to be guided by you. While she has her good friend who went through something terrible and they can share in their pain, it doesn't necessarily help with finding one's way. Therapy in this sense can mean the difference between going through the motions and living through them. Does that make sense? I do hope she continues to attend these meetings so she can come to terms with where she's been and how to get to where she wants to be. That's what I want for everyone who's been through something so terrible.

On another note, I know I'm always thanking you but (and I really do mean but), thank you. For what you said in the meeting and what you wrote below and for helping me to develop my strength. I know I've been through a nightmare but I truly feel like I am also living a dream. This could not be achieved without your influence.

If there was a choice to move backwards, believe me, I would do it in a minute. But it's not an option – so we move on with the pain and heartache that life as we knew it will never be the same."

Healing doesn't mean the damage never happened. It means the damage no longer controls your life. What and how you move forward is entirely up to you. It is in YOUR control. How and in which way you honour the memory of your loved one is in YOUR control. When/if/from whom you seek support is in YOUR control.

Grieve for me, for I would grieve for you.
Then brush away the sorrow and the tears.
Life is not over, but begins anew,
With courage you must greet the coming years.
To live forever in the past is wrong:
It can only cause you misery and pain.
Dwell not on memories overlong
With others you must share and care again.
Reach out and comfort those who comfort you,
Recall the years, but only for a while.
Nurse not your loneliness, but live again.
Forget not, but remember with a smile.

Navajo Prayer

So **Someone Died... Now What?**

Now you know.

I am so very sorry for your loss.

Corrie

REFERENCES

Albom, M. (1997). *Tuesdays with Morrie: An Old Man, a Young Man, and Life's Greatest Lesson.* New York: Doubleday.

Bowlby, J, (1980) Attachment and Loss Volume III: Loss: Sadness and Depression. Basic Books, Inc.

Brind, J & Wilkinson, T. (2008) -Religion Creative Ideas for Pastorial Litergy – Funeral, Thanksgiving and Memorial Services. Canterbury Press Norwich, London.

The Centre for the Grief Journey. (n.d.). *Laughter is Healthy.* Retrieved from http://www.griefjourney.com/wp/what-we-offer/for-professionals-and-caregivers/articles-for-professionals-and-caregivers/laughter-is-healthy/

Coelho, P. (2005). *Eleven Minutes.* New York: Perennial.

Coloroso, B. (1994). *Kids Are Worth It!: Giving Your Child the Gift of Inner Discipline.* New York: W. Morrow.

Coloroso, B. (2000). *Parenting through Crisis: Helping Kids in Times of Loss, Grief, and Change.* Toronto: HarperCollins.

Cook, J., & DuFalla, A. (2012). *Grief is Like a Snowflake.* Chattanooga, TN: National Center for Youth Issues.

Corr, C. A., Nabe, C. M. & Corr, D. (2003). *Death and Dying/Life and Living.* CA: Thomson Wadsworth.

Cousins, N. (2005). *Anatomy of an Illness as Perceived by the Patient.* New York: W.W. Norton.

Crenshaw, D. (1995). *Bereavement: Counseling the Grieving throughout the Life Cycle.* Crossroad Publishing Company.

Dalai, L., & Cutler, H. (1998). Transforming Suffering. In *The Art of Happiness: A Handbook for Living* (p. 146). New York: Riverhead Books.

DeSpelder, L. A. & Strickland, A. L. (2002). *The Last Dance*. Boston: McGraw-Hill.

Dyer, W. (2009). *There's a Spiritual Solution to Every Problem*. S.l.: HarperCollins.

Engel, L., & Ferguson, T. (1991). *Hidden Guilt*. New York: Pocket.

Ericsson, S. (1993). *Companion through the Darkness: Inner Dialogues on Grief* (p. 7). New York: Harper Perennial.

Grollman, E. (1993). Grief. In *Straight Talk about Death for Teenagers: How to Cope with Losing Someone You Love* (p. 6). Boston: Beacon Press.

Johnson, S. (2003). *The Present: The Gift That Makes You Happy and Successful at Work and in Life*. New York: Doubleday.

Kettering, T. (1989). *The Elephant in the Room*. Colorado: Bereavement Publishing Inc.

Kübler-Ross, E., & Kessler, D. (2005). Afterword: The Gift of Grief. In *On grief and grieving: Finding the meaning of grief through the five stages of loss* (p. 230). New York: Scribner.

Kübler-Ross, E. (1969). *On Death & Dying: What the Dying Have to Teach Doctors, Nurses, Clergy & Their Own Families*. New York: Scribner.

Kushner, H (2002). *When All You've Ever Wanted Isn't Enough: The Search for a Life That Matters*. New York: Simon and Schuster.

Linn, D. (1995). *Sacred Space: Clearing and Enhancing the Energy of Your Home*. New York: Ballantine Books.

Marron,D.(n.d.). Guilt. Retrieved from
http://www.sdpsychologist.com/special_report.htm

McGhee, P. (2002). How Humor Helps You Cope. Retrieved from
http://www.laughterremedy.com/articles.dir/articles_frame.html

Murakami, H. (2005). *Kafka on the Shore*. New York: Alfred A.
Knopf.

Novak, W., & Waldoks, M. (2006). *The Big Book of Jewish
Humor*. New York: HarperCollins.

Parkes, C. (1972). *Bereavement: Studies of Grief in Adult Life*.
London: Penguin.

Parkes, C. (2006). *Love and Loss: The Roots of Grief and its
Complications*. London: Routledge.

Pettibone Poole, M. (1938). *A Glass Eye at a Keyhole*.
Philadelphia, Dorrance and Company.

Picoult, J. (2005). *Vanishing Acts*. New York: Atria Books.

Rando, T. (1984). *Grief, Dying, and Death: Clinical Interventions
for Caregivers*. Illinois: Research Press.

Rando, T. (1991). *How To Go On Living When Someone You Love
Dies*. New York: Bantam.

Rasmussen, C. (2013, October 30). What Happens When We
Grieve. Retrieved from
http://psychcentral.com/blog/archives/2013/11/05/what-happens-
when-we-grieve/

Roth, V. (2012). *Insurgent*. New York: Katherine Tegen Books.

Schneider, J. (2012). *Finding My Way: From Trauma to
Transformation: The Journey Through Loss and Grief*. Traverse
City, Michigan: Seasons Press.

Schwalbe, W. (2013, January 28). The Loss Of A Loved One: How To Get Through It. Retrieved from http://www.huffingtonpost.com/2013/01/28/the-loss-of-a-loved-one-grief-death_n_2333427.html

Shaw, G. (1954). *The Doctor's Dilemma: A Tragedy*. Baltimore: Penguin Books.

Stoppard, T. (1967). *Rosencrantz & Guildenstern Are Dead*. New York: Grove Press.

Stroebe, M., Schut, H. (1995). *The Dual Process Model of Coping with Loss*. Paper presented at the International Workshop on Death, Dying and Bereavement, St. Catherine's College, Oxford, UK.

Swindoll, C. (1998) Retrieved from http://www.goodreads.com/author/quotes/5139.Charles_R_Swindoll

Turner, J. (2014). *Julia's Story: A Memoir*. Eve Paludan Books.

Webb, N. B. (2004). *Mass Trauma and Violence: Helping Families and Children Cope*. NY: Guilford Press.

Wolfelt, A. D. (1996). *Healing the Bereaved Child*. CO: Companion Press

Worden, J. W. (2001). *Children and Grief: When a Parent Dies*. NY: Guilford Press.

Worden, J. (2008). *Grief Counseling and Grief Therapy: A Handbook for the Mental Health Practitioner* (4th ed.). New York: Springer Publishing.

ABOUT THE AUTHOR

Corrie Sirota holds a Master of Social Work as well as a Graduate Certificate in Loss and Bereavement from McGill University (Montreal, Canada) where she has been a sessional lecturer in the School of Social Work for over twenty years. As a licensed psychotherapist, she maintains a private practice, specializing in loss and bereavement as well as non-death losses. Corrie is the clinical supervisor for the After Care Department of Paperman and Sons Funeral Home (Montreal, Canada) and a consultant for Chai Life Line (Montreal, Canada). She currently facilitates bereavement groups for widows, young adults, perinatal loss, and postpartum support.

As an expert in her field, Corrie presents regularly at conferences and workshops both locally and internationally, and often appears on radio and television news programs. She wrote "Helping Children Cope with Death" which appeared in the Jewish Funeral Directors Association magazine as well as in Living Legacies Volume III, 2011 and has authored numerous other articles and blog posts for ME Magazine, Cappino Physio and Wellness Centre, and Risk within Reason.

Corrie currently lives in Montreal with her husband and their two children.

Should you wish to contact Corrie to book a workshop or consultation, please visit her website: www.corriesirota.com.

Made in the USA
Charleston, SC
13 February 2016